BBQ&A

with **MYRON MIXON**

BBQ&A

with MYRON MIXON

WRITTEN WITH KELLY ALEXANDER

For my fans.

CONTENTS

With my Jack's Old South crew: Bill Wheeler,
TJ Wehunt, Michael Mixon, Tracy Mixon,
Tim Bolliger, Ed Harris, and Bobby Harman

INTRODUCTION

WELCOME TO MYRON MIXON'S ULTIMATE F.A.Q.

Got a burning question about barbecue? From all I've seen in my twenty-five years as a professional pitmaster, I know you have at least one question that's bugging you, at least one nagging issue that comes up every time you're getting ready to barbecue in your backyard. Well, you have come to the right place.

Y'all know what an "F.A.Q." is, right? It's that list of questions and answers that could be about any topic, and all of the questions are supposedly the ones that are the most commonly asked. You see an F.A.Q. in a new-product guide or in an online forum, and you see them on websites when you need customer service and support. Sometimes those questions are about very basic stuff, and other times they are super specific—but they just go to show you that explanations are necessary for just about every facet of American life these days. All of us consumers appreciate additional well-organized information about the topics that interest us. We've come to expect that we can get all our questions answered whenever we want to.

Barbecue is no different. Believe it or not, even the winningest man in barbecue—that's me, Myron Mixon—has a list of "frequently asked questions." These are the things people ask me over and over again . . . when I'm on the road competing in contests, or attending events to do smoking demos, or teaching barbecue cooking classes. Sometimes people shout these questions at me during barbecue contests. Other times they post them on my Facebook page or tweet them. And just like the questions in many instruction manuals, they range from the very general—"What does championship barbecue taste like?" (see page 24 for that one)—to the very precise—"How can I get a smoke ring to go all the way around my brisket?" (see page 228). Some questions are all about hogs: How do I smoke a whole hog if I've never done it before (see page 138)? Or: Is there an easy way to make great pulled pork (see page 159)? Others are about fixing common barbecue problems: Why does the skin on my chicken thighs come out rubbery (see page 112)? Then there are those that are a little odd: I can't figure out why people always want to know what I eat when I'm not eating barbecue (see a page in someone else's book, because my answer just ain't that interesting—I happen to like Italian food). And a surprising number of folks ask me if you can cook desserts in a smoker (you can; see page 311).

As a barbecue champion who travels all over the world for cooking competitions, TV appearances, and other events, I've kept track of all the various issues that come up over and over again for my fans. *I want you to think of BBQ&A as my ultimate F.A.Q.* For the first time ever, I'm going to answer the questions I commonly receive and provide exactly the recipes and instructions you want all in one place. In the upcoming pages I'll be answering more than a hundred of the barbecue-loving public's most frequently asked questions of me—in the process of offering up my smoking techniques and methods, barbecue flavors and meat preparations, and my best recipes and formulas.

Why am I doing this? *BBQ&A* is for all the people living what I call the "barbecue lifestyle." If you are from the South, where I've lived all my life, you probably already know what this means. Down here, barbecue is a career for some and a hobby for most. It's also a way of living. If you drive down a street in a suburban neighborhood like mine, you'll see in damn near every driveway or backyard a smoker—whether it's a big old rusty barrel, or a ceramic green one, or one of the sophisticated chest-style ones that the pros use. That smoker might be next to a fishing boat, or a pickup truck, or both. Over the years our barbecue way of life is something that has been catching on throughout the country, and now throughout the world. This book is for all of you in the growing army of folks out there who care deeply about making the world's best barbecue—I'm one of you. I know that we do it for a number of different reasons: to feed our families and friends, to win a contest, or just because it's what we do.

I told you that I hear from folks about their own barbecue efforts all the time, but it happens the most when I'm in my element competing in a barbecue contest. Especially at a big barbecue event, like one of the larger contests sponsored

Unadilla, Georgia

by the Kansas City Barbecue Society (KCBS) or the Memphis Barbecue Network: I'll have people come up to me and say that the reason they got into barbecue is because of me. I love that. Here's why: Most folks assume—can't blame them, it's because of what they hear me say on TV—that I'm just into competitive barbecue for the paycheck. Believe me, I do love that paycheck. But what gets me going, and the reason I still cook barbecue after all these years in the first place, are those comments from my fans, those pats on the back they give me when they tell me, **"Your barbecue is the best damn barbecue I've ever put in my mouth."** That's the greatest feeling in the world, right there.

No matter what our jobs are, I think all of us love to feel respected and appreciated. We are all looking for our next "Atta boy!" So we pitmasters are always striving to get that next pat on the back—from our friends, our families, our judges . . . hell, even from our enemies. We want that "great job" from anyone and everyone who eats barbecue. Make no mistake: Every pitmaster, from the backyard warriors on up to the grand champions, seeks the confirmation that his or her food tastes great. Once you get a taste of that acclaim for something you've cooked, you start craving it: You're always trying to get better at your cooking, you're practicing your techniques and recipes, and you're thinking and dreaming about barbecue. I want to keep my friends and family beyond happy with my food, and I want to keep my fans in awe. I have won so much and gotten so much attention for my cooking that I could walk away from the world of barbecue right now and never cook another hog (page 138), another brisket (page 223), another damn cupcake chicken (page 96), and I would be fine. But I'm not doing that. I'm as hooked on the barbecue lifestyle as the people who just bought their first smoker.

This book is for my fans, because their affirmation that my barbecue is the best ever is what has kept me going all these years. I love y'all.

Disclaimer: This book contains *my* answers to the questions most frequently asked of *me*, Myron Mixon. I am not a professional nutritionist, a home economist, an academic historian, or a scientist. I am a barbecue champion. What I can tell you is how I got that way, and how you can make food at home that tastes a lot like what I go out there every day and win contests by cooking. This is not the "ultimate guide to barbecue" that's going to tell you all about how they cook meat in Alabama versus how they do it in Thailand. This book is the ultimate guide to Myron Mixon's style of championship barbecue. And that ought to be enough to at least get you started.

MYRON'S BBQ&A

Before we get into the meat of the book, here are some questions and answers about my time on the competitive barbecue circuit.

Q:

Which competition is the most fun to compete in, and why?

A:

The Giant National Capital Barbecue Battle in Washington, DC, is a damn fine time. Why? You're cooking right on Pennsylvania Avenue, right down the street from the White House. No matter who you voted for, when you cook barbecue on Pennsylvania Avenue you're doing it near the president of the United States, which is pretty cool. The contest organizers shut down six blocks, and the pitmasters get to stand right on the street and smoke our hogs, pork shoulders, and briskets right there in full view of the U.S. government. I've had the mayor from DC come down, along with all kinds of Congress people. I'm just waiting for the president to show up someday.

Q:

Which contest has the largest purse?

A:

The Memphis in May World Championship Barbecue Cooking Contest is the one that'll net you the most money. If you can manage to win the grand championship, you're looking at $40,000. Now, you have other kinds of cooking contests these days where you can make even more money. For instance, you've got the World Food Championships, where grand champions of all kinds of previous events compete to win $100,000. But none of them means as much as winning Memphis in May. That's the most important one to me, and I've won it four times. As a member of my team, my son Michael has won, too. Now I'm waiting for him to win Memphis in May for himself, running his own crew.

Q:

How much have I won?

A:

Since 1996, I have won:
— More than 200 grand championships
— More than 30 state championships
— 11 national championships
— 4 world championships
— 9-time Memphis in May team of the year
— More than $1 million in prize money
— More than 1,800 trophies
— Induction into the Barbecue Hall of Fame, 2013
— Carolyn and Gary Wells "Pioneer of Barbecue" Award, 2018

Q:

Which contest was your first win?

A:

The first prizes I ever won for cooking barbecue were in 1996 at the Lock & Dam BBQ Contest in Augusta, Georgia. Guess what? It was the first contest I ever even entered. I took two first-place finishes—for whole hog and for ribs—and one third-place, for pork shoulder. That was pretty damn good for a first-timer. My first grand championship was at the Big Pig Jig. That contest has a special place in my heart. Not only is it one of the biggest barbecue contests in the Southeast, but also my dad was involved with it before he passed away—and it takes place in my hometown of Vienna, Georgia, where his original restaurant was. I won that contest in 1997 with my first grand championship, and then I won it again in 2013, almost twenty years later, when we filmed it for *BBQ Pit Wars*. Please believe me, I love whooping the asses of my competitors at the Big Pig Jig.

Q:

Which state championship is the most important to you, and why?

A:

For me, the state barbecue championship that means the most is naturally the one from the state of Georgia, my home state and where I still live. At one time before the world of competitive barbecuing became so popular, there used to be only one state championship in each state. Nowadays, there can be more than one—for example, the state of Kansas has something like fifty state championships. It does not make sense to me. Back in the day, the Big Pig Jig was the only barbecue championship in the state of Georgia. You had 140 teams competing against each other, cooking whole hogs. That kind of contest is the heart and soul of competitive barbecue.

I'll tell you another state contest I like: The Kentucky state championship is a fun one. One year when I was competing, the barbecue part was on Friday and Saturday, and on Sunday they were having a mutton contest. Now, normally I wouldn't mess with mutton—I did not grow up cooking and eating it. But I saw that it paid $2,000 to win the mutton portion of the contest. So even though I'd never cooked mutton in my life, I thought: What the hell, I'll give it a shot. I noticed that all the other competitors were cooking whole mutton, but I didn't know how to do that and I didn't have the time to practice. Instead, I went out and bought a lamb shoulder roast and some racks of lamb chops and gave it my best shot. There were forty teams that entered the mutton contest, many of whom had extensive knowledge of mutton and had been cooking mutton for years; that was my competition. But guess what? I won it. I took that big check, and then I got the hell out of there.

Was there ever a barbecue contest you were sure you'd lose?

I will never forget this one time when I was competing in the South Carolina Festival of Discovery Barbecue Contest in Greenwood, South Carolina. I was watching the finishes closely. It was a KCBS-sponsored event, which means there are four categories that you have to cook—chicken, ribs, pork shoulder, and brisket. The good news was that we'd placed in all four. The bad news was that we'd gotten a sixth, an eighth, a ninth, and an eleventh. I was watching a whole bunch of other teams collect their first-, second-, and third-place prizes, just knowing that our team was done, that we were out of the contest for sure. Guess what? We ended up winning the grand championship! Turns out that even though a bunch of other teams placed higher than we did in individual categories, none of the rest of them scored in all four. I was shocked. More fun than me being in shock, though, was looking around at everybody else being like, "How did that just happen?"

Did you ever compete in a contest that you were just sure you were going to win, but then lost?

A:

Oh yes, unfortunately. I was competing in a KCBS contest three years ago. We had won two first-place finishes and a third, and I just knew the grand championship was going to be ours. All we had to do was wait for our brisket score to come in before we could collect the prize. Guess what? We wound up finishing something like fourth or fifth overall. What happened? We got a low score on our brisket—which was underserving, I might add—and that sunk the championship for us. I would also like to add that I've won that particular contest thirteen times. But I don't have hard feelings.

Q:

which contest is toughest?

A:

The hardest contest to compete in is also the contest where I have the most experience, and that's the Memphis in May World Championship. First of all, it's a contest where you can cook whole hog (page 144), a skill that attracts only the best teams. To me, cooking a whole hog is a true test of a pitmaster's abilities. It's hard work. You don't come to a contest to cook and party and choose whole hog as your category. At Memphis in May, you only choose one category to compete in. People who come there to party—and I don't blame them, it's a big, fun party for sure—do not cook whole hog. Those competitors cook ribs—and that's easy, because all you have to do is come out to the grounds early on Saturday morning, smoke your ribs for three hours, and then turn them in. You're done, and you can go party. But cooking a hog is a two-day process. In any

year you've got forty or fifty teams cooking whole hogs, and all of us have got to stay up all night doing it. That's dedication.

Q:

what's up with the oversize checks they give you when you win a barbecue contest?

A:

People ask me about those oversize prize checks sometimes. Guess what? They're symbols, and they're worth the paper they're printed on. The real winnings come to you as soon as thirty days or as late as ninety days after the contest—unless you can do something I've never been able to do, which is find a bank that'll cash a gigantic cardboard check.

True story: The first time I agreed to work with a publisher on a cookbook, I had a big conference call with the editors. At some point in that call they asked me what was most important to me about the upcoming project, and I told them that I was good as long as I got one of those big checks—but I had no idea how they would mail it from New York City to Georgia. The call got real quiet then. I don't think some of those New Yorkers realized I was messing with them, at least for a couple of minutes.

Q:

Who is the most famous person you've met at a barbecue contest?

A:

People ask me this a lot, too. I've met some famous people. I guess one of the biggest thrills was meeting Joe Perry of Aerosmith. Dale Earnhardt, Jr., is a fan of mine, and that's pretty damn cool. And I've met many other celebrity chefs, like Guy Fieri, and even went on a USO tour with Adam Richman from *Man v. Food* to South Korea. And I've met countless athletes (I got to cook for the Atlanta Falcons recently) and many politicians.

Q:

What is your favorite meat to cook in a competition?

A:

I love cooking a whole hog. I like cooking whole hog better than anything else in the world, to tell you the truth. Everything about it is second nature to me. If you want to be an honest-to-god pitmaster, you have to master the whole hog. And I like being able to show off the fact that I can cook a damn-near perfect whole hog, in contest after contest. It's very rewarding to smoke a whole hog, too, because after you're done you get to eat something that tastes close to heaven. My second-favorite thing to cook is brisket. Why? Because I cooked pork all my life, and brisket is something different; it's a challenge to get it right, and I had to learn how to do it. I love to eat beef, and smoking a brisket is rewarding for me in an entirely different way (page 222).

Q:

What is your least favorite competition category?

A:

How fast can I answer this? Chicken. Still and always, I have never really enjoyed smoking chicken. Why? Number one, it's a piece of meat that judges scrutinize tougher than they do the meat in any other category. For example, they check to make sure that your chicken thighs are all sized identically—and it's a real pain to make that happen. Chicken is also less flavorful than pork or beef, and to get good scores for cooking it, the judges like to see the newest, latest, greatest sauce on the chicken. The flavors they're looking for with chicken change all the time—sweet and tangy one year, mesquite-flavored another year. I hate keeping up with trends like that.

Q:

Who are all the guys helping you at contests?

A:

My blackshirts, the Jack's Old South crew who work with me and help me in all my contests (and wear the signature team-sponsored all-black collared button-downs when they're cooking with me, hence the nickname), I love all of those guys. Tracy Mixon, my brother, was with me learning at the hot pits with our father, and he's my right-hand man today. I'm also very proud of my son Michael. My other kids are all doing great with what they do, but Michael is trying to follow in my footsteps and in my dad's footsteps. Bill Wheeler is the smartest guy in my crew—there is nothing he cannot fix—and he knows how to cook, too. Ed Harris has been with me a long time and is as reliable a man as I've met. And, of course, Faye Mixon is my favorite person in the world of barbecue and beyond, because I couldn't be Myron without her.

Q:

What's your advice to pitmasters who are just starting out?

A:

Let me tell you what. When I started cooking competitive barbecue, you didn't get paid anything to be team of the year. We just competed for the love of barbecue. Now everybody thinks that they're gonna win a title, or they're gonna get rich cooking barbecue. Everybody wants to duplicate what I've done. They want to be on TV, and create their own rubs and sauces, and do appearances and receive licensing fees, and write books—they want to do it all. It ain't just about cooking for them. What I want to tell folks interested in going into competitive barbecue is that you have got to be able to have a presence. You have got to be able to speak knowledgeably about barbecue before you can do anything else. You have to know enough, and cook well enough, to win contests. And then you have to be articulate enough to explain what you're doing to judges. You have to wrap your heads around the fact that barbecue ain't just about winning a contest. You gotta be interesting. You gotta know what you're talking about, you gotta learn your craft, and you gotta be able to speak about it in a way that you don't sound like a fool. Why should anyone listen to me? Cook my barbecue, read my books—you'll know. My work speaks for itself. And your goal should be making sure yours does, too.

CHAPTER ONE

THE THRILL OF VICTORY

Myron Mixon's Brisket
page 223

Championship
St. Louis Ribs
page 189

Smoked
Half Chickens
page 107

Q:

What is the difference between competition cooking and what I cook in my backyard?

A:

I became a competitive pitmaster after my father passed away unexpectedly in 1996. Before that, I had spent my entire childhood, or so it seemed to me, helping my dad at his barbecue pits, and I wanted nothing to do with cooking barbecue for a career. But life has a funny way of surprising you. After my dad's untimely passing, I had to take over his business of making and selling barbecue sauce from a recipe that came from my mother's side of the family. At first, contests for me were just a new platform for selling sauce. Then I noticed the prize money and got to counting: I could promote our barbecue sauce, *and if I figured out how to win those contests*, I could make some money on the side, too. When people ask me about "competition barbecue," what it tastes like, and how it's different from backyard barbecue—well, that's what I had to figure out for myself.

A good way to think about it is like one of those Venn diagrams: Imagine two interlocking circles. In one circle there's competition barbecue, and in the other there's backyard barbecue. In the middle, between the two, are what they have in common. That's what you want to go for when you're cooking at home: Backyard barbecue that is more "professional"—and by that I mean that it looks better and tastes more delicious—than what your neighbor's cooking.

There are two main organizations that sanction barbecue contests: Memphis Barbecue Network and Kansas City Barbecue Society (KCBS). The contests themselves have some differences—for example, Memphis contests are whole hog, with on-site judge visits, while KCBS contests allow brisket and other meats and are blind-box judging only. But back when I got involved in competition barbecue, most folks who were into it were hobbyists—it wasn't like it is now, where folks have figured out how to be professional pitmasters. So, I was on my own to figure out what the judges liked. These barbecue judges look for *taste*, *tenderness*, and *appearance*. When it comes to taste, judges want first and foremost for the meat to taste like meat. Sometimes I have to remind the students at my cook schools that barbecue contests are *meat* contests—smoked hog should taste like hog, not grape jelly. Also, there's a difference between smoked food and food that tastes too smoky: You want the meat's own flavor to be enhanced by smoke, and not the other way around. Tenderness follows straight from taste. Texture is extremely important when it comes to barbecue. If you don't know what you're doing, it's almost too easy to dry out your meat. Appearance: Judges are looking for "eye appeal"—does what's in front of them look good enough to eat? The judges ask themselves: Is it attractive, does it have appropriate and good-looking garnishes, and if it's supposed to have certain visual features (like a smoke ring on a brisket; see page 228), are they there?

I'm not going to lie to you: There are differences between competition barbecue and backyard barbecue. At contests, judges have certain trends they seem to like to see in the food—I've heard it said that judges prefer barbecue on the saucy and sweet side, and in a lot of cases I've found that to be true. Do you need to worry about that? You do not. Focus on the main attributes I told you about—taste, tenderness, and appearance—and when the time comes to barbecue in your own backyard, you'll do just fine.

Q:

What does championship barbecue taste like?

A:

The best barbecue in the world tastes like barbecue. I don't know how else to answer this question (and I get it a fair amount) except to remind you folks that barbecue is first and foremost a simple cooking technique. All you're doing is cooking meat over fire. And what that's supposed to taste like when you're done is a tender meat that's moist in your mouth with layers of flavor that come from the mild and delicate nature of the meat itself and the aromas of the smoke that circulate around it while it cooks. Do not make this process more complicated than it needs to be, people. You marinate the meat to tenderize it and soften it and add a layer of flavor. You rub the meat with spices to further enhance those flavors. You cook the meat at a low temperature over hot coals to both seal in those flavors and add a final dimension of earthy smokiness. That's it. Keep that in mind while you're cooking and you can turn out championship barbecue in your backyard. The bottom line is that although this is a simple cooking technique, there is a definitely a way to do it right. If you don't take learning how to cook barbecue seriously, your food is not going to taste good. The good news is that if you respect the fact that there's a "right" way to do this, and you have the desire to learn about how to do it to the best of your abilities, you're going to be the king of your neighborhood.

Q:

What's the difference between smoking on a smoker and smoking on a pit? And: What is the difference between grilling, barbecuing, smoking, and pit-smoking?

A:

These are excellent questions. Most people think of "barbecuing" as just one way of cooking, as just one technique, but it's more complicated than that. In a way, these questions are also about equipment: If you can be patient, I'm going to break down all of the types of grills, smokers, and cookers for you (if you just can't wait, turn to page 40).

The thing you need to know here is that barbecue came about because there was a need for the people who first came to this country in its earliest days to be able to feed themselves simply and cheaply. Now, folks have been cooking meat over fire since the beginning of time, of course, and barbecuing is just one very well-known evolution of that process. You also need to know the difference between barbecuing and grilling. Grilling involves cooking food directly over a source of heat—an open flame—over high heat, like 350 to 400°F and even higher. Grilling is ideal for searing tender pieces of meat, like most cuts of steak, boneless skinless chicken breasts, and pork tenderloin. Lots of men and women are good at it and I'm one of them, but my life is devoted to something different.

My life is all about barbecuing. Yes, both grilling and barbecuing are methods that involve cooking outside and managing fires. But the similarities to what I'm doing and grilling end there. I specialize in true barbecuing (otherwise known as *smoking* and), which not only cooks the meat at 350°F or lower but also infuses and tenderizes the meat with smoke and other natural flavors that can only come from cooking food by means of indirect wood-fired heat. Because the foods cook slowly and at a low temp, it's good to smoke the ones that need a longer time to tenderize—like brisket, pork shoulder, and ribs. (Not that you can't smoke steaks and chicken breasts, mind you—you can pretty much smoke anything you can grill, but remember that you can't grill everything you can smoke.) Pit smoking involves cooking everything in a masonry pit that is fired by coals you make yourself out of fresh wood. That may sound intimidating, but it's a very easy and inexpensive process—I wrote a whole book about it called *Myron Mixon's BBQ Rules* that I encourage you to explore, including giving instructions for building a pit in your backyard for about $300. In that book I also explain the very "old-school" process of pit cooking, which is how I first learned to barbecue from my daddy. It boils down to cooking on a homemade coal-fired masonry pit, where the first step is burning down wood to make your own coals, then shoveling those coals beneath the meat, and finally cooking that meat over direct heat. This is an ancient form of cooking that came from the time that the forefathers of this country first started barbecuing. These gentlemen— and women, too—were trying to feed large families and do it cheaply with what they had. They took the livestock they had on the farms, and they took the trees they had surrounding them as their fuel to get the wood they needed to burn for their fires, and they used as ingredients the things they had on the farm for seasoning. Don't forget that.

Using a smoker? My first realization that coal-fired pit barbecue was a throwback to a bygone era was not until I was in my teens and started noticing that everybody but us had these offset smokers, the kind of metal cookers like the ones I use now. That's downright technological to folks like me. And that's what this book is about—how to make the best meat in the world by cooking it over smoking coals in your smoker. When you come from where I come from, learning how to use a smoker is actually considered *easier* than other forms of cooking. If you're feeling anxious about using your smoker, you can try to look at it that way, too.

How many kinds of barbecue are there, really?

I'm a professional pitmaster but an amateur barbecue historian— so please know that I'm not giving you the world's most thorough encyclopedia-style account here. What I can do is tell you about the major styles of barbecue that I'm familiar with and give you a little bit of information on what makes each style unique. Let's begin by agreeing on what barbecue is: meat cooked on a framework over an open fire, at a low temperature in a closed smoker or pit.

That's settled. Here is how I distinguish between the major styles:

IN THE UNITED STATES

American barbecue is most often divided into four major categories. Now, within these categories there are subcategories. For example, Georgia barbecue, which is *my* style, is similar to eastern Carolina vinegar-based barbecue. Folks in Tennessee like to have their ribs dry, with no sauce on them. You get the idea. Note that these are all massive generalizations: You can find barbecue without a hint of sugar in the sauce in Kansas, and you can also find good ribs in Texas. And of course you can find chicken in all of them. But this is about how things stack up:

Carolina barbecue: Pork is the supreme meat for Carolinians in both states, and it's usually the shoulder they're smoking. A lot of pitmasters make "pulled pork" by tearing handfuls of tender smoked shoulder meat into soft threads. Others chop that tender smoked shoulder meat into tiny pieces with a cleaver and pile them on rolls for barbecue sandwiches. In terms of sauces, North Carolina is a state divided: In the eastern part of the state, folks like thin vinegar-based sauce flavored with red pepper flakes; in the western part of the state, folks add tomato sauce or ketchup to that mixture. In the southern part of the state and in South Carolina, people favor mustard-based yellow barbecue sauce, sometimes sweetened with a little honey or molasses.

Memphis barbecue: The hog's the thing in Memphis, too, and to their beloved shoulder category they also add ribs. They love those in Memphis, and they like their meat dry—which doesn't mean "dry" in this case but rather, with no sauce. Cooks apply a thick rub to their shoulders and ribs, smoke them, and then sprinkle them with a little more rub before serving them—that's a Memphis dry rib.

Kansas City barbecue: Like Memphis, Kansas City is one of barbecue's most hallowed grounds. Pork is a big deal here, too, including ribs and shoulders. And they like ribs, both spare and baby back. But they also like beef and brisket, and they lay claim to inventing "burnt ends"—the crisp, charred ends of smoked briskets. The defining feature of KC barbecue is their thick and sweet sauce, which is tomato-based and often sweetened with brown sugar, corn syrup, or molasses.

Texas barbecue: Texans love to barbecue beef, and they prize the cut of brisket above all others. Wood and smoke are the primary flavors they use—they keep it simple, and they do that because they also like somewhat thick tomato-based sauces served along with the meat. They usually slice their barbecue—instead of chopping it—and they like it with soft white bread, or "Texas toast," on the side.

AROUND THE WORLD

Australian barbecue: Australian barbecue—like Crocodile Dundee throwing some *shrimp on the barbie*—is grilling. Cooks grill meat directly over the glowing embers in their grill. And they use "table grills" that are often long and narrow with a grate mounted on top of them and resting on a trolley platform or legs. And the meats they like to grill are usually lamb, sausages, crawfish and prawns, and, yes, shrimp.

Japanese barbecue: What the Japanese are best known for are their hibachi grills. They are small portable charcoal grills designed for high heat, with built-in air vents to control the heat. They're great for kebabs, teriyaki, and other seasoned and marinated small cuts and cubes of meat.

Argentinean barbecue: The term "barbecue" comes from the Spanish word *barbacoa*, which was originally used to describe the cooking structure of a cauldron suspended over a fire pit. South Americans love their barbecue, and their traditional *asado* feast is a like a big ol' mixed grill to feed a whole community. The meats, sausages, and offal they prepare are on big metal cross-like skewers stuck in the ground and surrounded by smoking charcoal or an open fire. It's cool.

"Let's begin by agreeing on what barbecue is: meat cooked on a framework over an open fire, at a low temperature in a closed smoker or pit."

Q:

What's your favorite kind of barbecue?

A:

People ask me this all the time, and to be honest with you, I think it's a ridiculous question. I like all food that tastes good and is well prepared, and I like all sorts of food. When it comes to barbecue, I have a lot of different kinds of favorites. Brisket is special to me because I had to learn how to cook it right—I wasn't born knowing how, so to speak. Ribs are special to me because I've won world championships with them. But I have to say overall that whole hog is my number one. I love to cook it, and I sure love to eat it. The reason I like it so much is that it requires the most skill to cook. Not even all pitmasters—I would say probably not even half of the young pitmasters I've run across in my life—know how to smoke a whole hog or have any clue as to how to go about it. It is the ultimate test of a cook's technique at the smoker—his or her ability to manage all the various cuts in the whole animal, his or her use and management of seasonings and flavors, and his or her patience and diligence at seeing a long and involved process all the way through to the end. Whole hog is the endurance sport of cooking, and at the end you are so very well rewarded. Nothing else can compete.

What's the easiest kind of barbecue to cook?

The easiest kind of barbecue to cook is the one that somebody else made, of course. Ain't nothing wrong with getting barbecue takeout in my book, because that's the business that supported my family when I was growing up—and god bless it. But when people ask me about this, I think they're looking for something that's not only simple to make but also *fast*. People are always looking for shortcuts in our day and age, and most of the time I'm no different. I don't like a lot of worriation on a busy weeknight, either. I've got two go-to recipes that are extremely easy. One of them is for high-heat grilling of a thick and juicy porterhouse steak (page 32), and it won't take you more than half an hour from start to finish. The other is for very simple smoked whole chicken that has three ingredients (page 33)—you set it up, put it in the smoker, and if you play your cards right, three hours later you'll have a delicious dinner.

EASY GRILLED PORTERHOUSE STEAK

Two things to know: A porterhouse combines two cuts that are separated by a bone—there's tenderloin on one side and sirloin on the other. You want to spend a little dough for quality meat here, because that's one of the secrets of a great grilled steak—if you don't start out with something high quality, how do you expect to end up with something that's high quality when you're finished cooking? The second thing to keep in mind: You get that good seared crust on the steak only when the grill is very hot, so mind your temp.

ingredients

1 (2-pound) porterhouse steak, at least 1½ inches thick

1 recipe Beef Marinade (page 68)

Kosher salt, to taste

Freshly ground black pepper, to taste

Use paper towels or a clean kitchen towel to pat the steak dry all over. Place the steak in a gallon-size zip-top bag, pour in the beef marinade, and marinate the steak at room temperature for at least 2 hours. (Note: You can do this step before you go off to work in the morning and let the steak marinate in the fridge all day, that's no problem—more time in the marinade than that, though, and you risk soggy steak.)

When you're ready to cook the steak, prepare your grill with coals that are hot to very hot, 450 to 500°F.

Remove the steak from the marinade, discard the marinade, and use paper towels or a clean kitchen towel to thoroughly pat the steak dry. Season the steak liberally on both sides with salt and pepper.

Place the steak on the grill rack and sear it over direct heat for 6 to 9 minutes per side for medium rare, or until an instant-read thermometer registers 130°F. Transfer the steak to a wood cutting board or a platter, cover it with aluminum foil, and let it rest for 10 minutes.

When you're ready to serve the steak, uncover it. The best way to carve the steak: Use a sharp chef's knife to cut the bone out of the center (save it someplace safe for yourself so you can gnaw on it later), and then cut the meat across the grain in thick diagonal slices. You want each eater to get some of the meat from each side of the porterhouse.

EASY SMOKED CHICKEN

SERVES 2 TO 4

ingredients

1 (3½-pound) whole chicken

1 cup Jack's Old South Original Rub or make your own (see page 73)

2 cups water

1 cup Jack's Old South Hickory Sauce or make your own (see page 77)

Prepare your smoker and heat it to 275°F.

Apply the rub all over the exposed areas of the chicken and into the chicken's cavity as well. Place the seasoned bird with its breast side up on a meat rack with handles down, so the bird will be raised above the surface of a pan. Then set the rack inside a deep aluminum baking pan. Pour water into the bottom of the pan, underneath the meat rack. Carefully transfer the pan into the smoker, cover, and smoke for about 3 hours, or until the breast meat reaches a temperature of 165°F and the dark meat reaches 180°F.

Remove the pan from the smoker and allow the chicken to rest on its rack in the pan, uncovered, for 15 minutes. Transfer the chicken to a wooden carving board, carve the chicken into pieces, and serve with the sauce on the side.

Why should I attend a barbecue contest? How do barbecue contests work? How do I get started in competitive barbecue?

I'm asked this question or some variation of it all the damn time. Let me break it down into steps for you. This is a good plan for how to get involved in the world of competitive barbecue, assuming that's what you have your heart set on. I'll be seeing you at the comps:

1. **Get to know your cooker.** Learn how to prepare your fire, how to stoke it, and how to manage the heat. Start off with something simple: It's far easier to learn how to smoke meat with a cooker that's not too complicated. As your skills increase, you can always upgrade. In my experience, folks who start with something that has more bells and whistles on it than my world championship–winning rig almost always flame out.

2. **Develop a relationship with a good local butcher.** High-quality meats going on the smoker means high-quality food coming off it—it's that simple. Get to know your cuts and meats to the best of your ability and you'll be a better cook for it all around, whether you're at the smoker or the stove.

3. **Study up on barbecue flavors.** What do I mean by that? Learn about rubs, sauces, glazes, and injections. You can take a class—I recommend one of mine, of course. You can read recipe books—I recommend one of mine, of course. And you can make it your business to taste as much barbecue as you can, figure out what you like, and start developing your own style. Start attending some barbecue contests to see what they're like. Walk around, see how the competitors are working, taste as much food as you can, get the feel of the scene.

At the Windy City Smokeout in Chicago

4. Choose a contest. Sanctioned contests are better organized, better attended, and have better prize money. You know I don't mess around, so that's what I recommend. There are three main contest sanctioning bodies: the Kansas City Barbecue Society (KCBS), the Memphis Barbecue Network (MBN), and the International Barbecue Cookers Association (IBCA). Bigger contests have "open" and "invitation" sections. "Open" means teams who pay the entry fee ($150 and up) can compete; "invitation" means you have to be invited to participate—these generally have fewer competitors. If you see the word "qualifier," it means the contest's overall grand champion will qualify for the American Royal Invitational and have his or her team's name placed in the Jack Daniels World Championship Invitational Barbecue contest pool or the Memphis in May World Championship Barbecue Cooking Contest. Take it from me: Getting into those contests is an honor and a privilege. But for right now, your job is to study the available contests near you. Then I suggest to folks who are just getting started to go for a small one—you'll have better luck, and you'll get to know the competition routine better in a more intimate

The Thrill of Victory

setting. And remember that you don't have to enter all of the categories, either: Try for a couple of them just to get your feet wet. If you don't enter all the categories, you won't be eligible for grand or reserve champion, but in your first few contests that ain't gonna matter.

5. **Check the contest's rules and regulations very carefully.**
All of the contests are a little different, and they're all very particular. Read all the fine print. You would be surprised by how many folks I've seen spend a lot of money up front to compete in a barbecue contest only to discover that they arrived with the wrong materials or otherwise inadvertently violated the rules. Read the rules on garnish especially carefully—some contests allow a small cup of sauce, others allow fresh herbs and lettuce, and still others say no garnish at all. For the sake of all that's holy, don't get disqualified for breaking a garnish rule after you've smoked ribs to the best of your ability! KCBS contests usually have four main categories: chicken, ribs (loin or spare), pork (shoulder, picnic, or butt), and brisket. MBN contests have three main pork-only categories: whole hog, whole pork shoulder or fresh ham, and pork ribs. Many contests have a "fun" category, too, called "Anything But"—which means what it sounds like . . . you can enter anything but smoked beef, pork, or chicken. These are a great way to earn a little money by smoking or grilling anything you like.

Now you're good to go. Make yourself a packing list far in advance, check it twice, and bring twice as many aluminum pans, zip-top bags, cutting boards, and paper towels as you think you'll need. Don't forget the duct tape—you never know.

*How can I make my barbecue
taste better than anybody else's?*

That's what this book is for. That's what all my books, classes, and TV shows are for—to try to teach you how to make the best barbecue possible. But I'll give you a clue as to the secret ingredient: It's confidence. Like any other skill in the world, from sports to playing a musical instrument, the more you practice, the better you get. It sounds basic, I know, but it's very true when it comes to barbecue. Get out there in your backyard every weekend practicing, smoking shoulders and chicken and ribs, inviting over friends and family to taste your food and give you feedback (even if you only nod politely while they're giving it to you), and you'll get the hang of it. And once you get the hang of it, it's not that big a step to get good at it. People ask me why I don't mind sharing my recipes and cooking techniques with people. They say, "Don't you worry they'll be able to beat you?" I'll tell you one thing no one can beat me on: I've spent more hours cooking barbecue at my smoker than just about anybody else in the world. It's that practice and those hours and days and years that enable me to be the best.

CHAPTER TWO

GET THE SMOKIN' STARTED

'CUE BASICS & EQUIPMENT

Q:

what kind of grill
or smoker should I buy?

A:

The single best piece of advice I can give folks about equipment is this: You do *NOT* need expensive equipment to cook delicious barbecue. All the latest and greatest technological bells and whistles don't make the food taste good—it's the techniques you use and the flavors you're able to create that does it. Does a great machine help you achieve that? Yes, it certainly can. But before you go parting with thousands of dollars on a top-of-the-line smoker, I suggest that you practice on some lower-rent equipment. Once you start getting some techniques down, and you start figuring out times and temps for cooking your meats, you can think about upgrading. In fact, why don't you start off using what you've got: Most homeowners in America already own some type of grill or smoker. When it comes to gas or charcoal, know this: Almost all the folks in the world of professional barbecue favor charcoal cookers for grilling. They produce a clean, high heat that you just can't get with propane. There's an economic reason, too: Equipment for charcoal grilling is much cheaper—this is close to the method the earliest folks who cooked meat over fire used, and they sure weren't using gas.

MYRON'S GRILL & SMOKER 101

GAS GRILL

Gas grills: The most popular choice among all outdoor cookers is a gas grill, fueled by propane—Americans buy these the most. Nothing beats the convenience factor here. Gas grills are great because they're easy—you turn them on, they heat up, you cook your food, and you're done. It's pretty much no muss, no fuss. I know, I have a couple of gas grills in my compound, a.k.a. my training ground, where I practice my own recipes and techniques and where I teach all my barbecue cooking classes. You got push-button ignition, steady flowing heat that you don't have to worry too much about controlling, and ease of cleaning. What you miss by using a gas grill is pretty obvious: You don't get that great smoky flavor that's pretty much essential to barbecue because you're not burning wood and creating charcoals to smoke your food. Besides that, people who love their gas grills don't want for much: I've even got a method for adapting a gas grill for smoking that works great (see page 46).

KETTLE GRILL

Kettle grills: I've heard it said that kettle grills combine the technique of grilling with the technique of barbecuing in a single solitary device, and I agree with that idea. No wonder so many folks have these and love them, including me. The best-known brand is, of course, Weber, but there are others out there, too. Kettle grills have deep round bases that allow for them to be converted easily into devices that can roast or barbecue, and they have a grill grate that allows for cooking food over very hot, direct heat, too. These are the most basic cookers—inexpensive and easy to use. The big drum holds the heat, and the air vent helps you regulate it. Simple.

CHARCOAL GRILLS OR "SMOKERS"

Bullet smoker

Kamado-style smoker

off-set smoker

Charcoal grills or "smokers": A "smoker" is not one generic all-encompassing piece of equipment; in fact, there's an incredible range. Now there are electric and charcoal versions of **bullet smokers**, those tall vertical numbers that are sometimes called water smokers because they have compartments, and a water pan rests between the heat source and the grates. One issue with the vertical bullet smokers is that the surface area tends to be small, but they're still good to use for smaller pieces of meat. There are ceramic **kamado-style cookers** like the Big Green Egg. Most folks don't know that these have been around for thousands of years and were invented and popularized in Japan. The big pro to these is that they're very heavily insulated, which makes them very efficient at using a little fuel to hold maximum heat. Some teams use these in competitions and they can perform very well. The biggest issue with them is cost: I hesitate to recommend such an expensive piece of equipment to folks who are just learning how to smoke. And there are bigger competition-style smokers, the kind that fit on rigs. For example, **stick burners** are cookers that use wood not only to generate smoke but also as the primary heat source. This is for barbecue purists, and the smoky flavor they can be used to create is unbeatable. But this is also for advanced smokers: Stick burning technique requires the ability to master your fire, to know how to tend your pit and keep your cooker at a consistent temp over many hours of cooking. Finally, **pellet smokers** combine electricity with wooden pellets. Food-grade pellets are available in traditional "wood flavors" like oak, hickory, and peach, and you can set the thermostat on these suckers and then walk away.

HOW DO SMOKERS WORK?

They work like this: You use a charcoal "chimney" to start a fire with your hardwood charcoal. Then you use a long-handled grill spatula to push the coals over to one half of the grill. On one half you'll have hot coals. On the opposite side of the bottom of the grill from the hot coals, carefully place a disposable aluminum pan filled with water. Put your aromatic hardwood chunks, sticks, chips, or pellets on top of the hot coals. Place your grill grate on top, and you're ready to start smoking.

WHAT COOKER DO I RECOMMEND?

A *Myron Mixon Smoker*, of course. For years I have worked on designing a line of smokers myself, with the goal of creating the kind of cookers that I would've liked to have used when I first got started cooking barbecue in competitions. When I designed a cooker, the number-one thing that I wanted was to build one where you didn't need to keep opening it up all the time to check on your meat. I wanted a cooker that had evenly dispersed temperature, which is not an easy thing to manage when you're dealing with live fire. I asked myself: How can I keep as much of that precious smoke as possible inside the cooking chamber? That's every pitmaster's goal, by the way. So now I have a range of different models of smokers, but all of them rely on "water pan technology," which is what I credit for making my smokers the best on the market. The water pan helps maintain a consistent temperature in the smoker by circulating the heat evenly, which tenderizes the meat through the cooking process and also helps the meat retain its natural moisture. My water pan technology eliminates the complaints about "hot spots" that people have with other smokers, and also reduces fuel consumption. It's a very forgiving process. I also have dampers on either side of my fireboxes to help you control your heat.

THE MYRON MIXON SMOKER

*Can I make good barbecue
without a smoker or a pit?*

Yes, you can. In fact, you have my guarantee that if you follow my instructions, you can make good barbecue on a gas grill. Most gas grills have either two or three burners, and the burners can be controlled individually. That's great for folks who want to do some smoking, because it means you can set up indirect heat. Here are the steps you need to follow:

1. Take a big handful of your favorite wood chips (see page 50) and soak them in bowl of water overnight.

2. When you're ready to start cooking, drain the chips and then wrap them in foil, creating a packet. Poke a few holes in the top of the packet. Set the packet aside.

3. If you're using a two-burner gas grill: Light only one side. If you're using a three-burner grill: Light the two outside burners and leave the middle one cold.

4. Place the packet of soaked wood chips on the lit section (or sections). The flame will smolder the wet chips, producing smoke for your meat.

5. Place the meat on the unlit section and smoke it, following your recipe's instructions for timing and temp.

Note: Don't worry too much about the side vents on your gas grill. You won't be able to get them closed airtight, so just shut them as tightly as you can. Nobody's smokers are airtight anyway, not even the ones that belong to the pros.

Can I make good barbecue without a smoker or a grill?

Are you asking me if you can smoke food in an oven? You can't exactly smoke, no. But there are three things you can do to approximate the process, and they all work well and produce delicious—if not exactly "smoky" in the traditional sense—food.

Grill pans: The heavy cast-iron-skillet-type grill pans, with the raised ridges on the bottom that create grill marks, really work. They are built to conduct and hold high heat, and so if you oil them up well and get your gas or electric burner nice and hot, they can produce good steaks, burgers, grilled chicken breasts, and grilled thick-fleshed fish fillets. There's no live fire, which is what makes grilled foods really *sing* in your mouth, but if it's rainy outside or it's a Tuesday night and you just don't feel like firing up your cooker and hanging around outside to manage your fire, then I think a good high-quality grill pan is a pretty darn good investment. If you use a good grill pan, make sure you clean it thoroughly before and after each use, which will prevent the foods from sticking to it when you're cooking. To oil the bottom of the pan properly: Heat it over the burner and get it nice and hot. Get yourself about ¼ cup vegetable oil and either paper towels or a clean kitchen towel—fold the towel or towels into quarters to make a square "pad." Using long-handled tongs, dip the towel pad in the oil and rub it all over the bottom of the pan. Easy. One last thing: I find that marinating my meats very well in advance—taking the full twenty-four hours, for example, instead of just three or four—makes whatever I cook on my grill pan taste a lot better.

Stovetop smoking is an interesting method created to allow cooks to try to get true smoked flavor into their foods—by cooking indoors. Is it possible? Sure. Is it preferable to smoking outdoors? I don't think so, not to me. But is it good for folks who live in apartments and can't smoke outdoors, or for when your cookout is rained out? It is. There are two ways: You can buy a "stovetop smoker" set, which is essentially a large square stainless-steel pan that comes with a grate and a lid that slides over the top—it's basically a sealed box with a grate inside. You place hardwood sawdust or wood chips (packaged with these smokers) in the bottom of the pan, a drip tray and food grate go above it, and you cook over the front and back burners of your stove using low heat to ignite the wood and generate a small amount of smoke, which you then trap inside the pan with the tight-fitting lid so that the food inside absorbs it. They work best with small pieces of meat, for obvious reasons, but they work.

You can make your own stovetop smoker, and you can do that quite easily. This is a cool method for indoor smoking that works well for chicken thighs and breasts, fish fillets, pork chops, and pork loins. You need: a large stockpot, a metal steamer insert, aluminum foil, and wood chips or shavings. Here's what you do:

STOVETOP SMOKING

1. Line the bottom of the big heavy pot with a piece of foil. A big square piece is fine. You don't need to be too exact about it—just try to cover the bottom of the pot as best you can.

2. Sprinkle a few tablespoons of wood shavings on top of the foil. Look for "stovetop smoker chips" if you want to buy them, or make your own by shaving some off your hardwood.

3. Top with another layer of aluminum foil to cover the wood shavings. On top of that, put in the steamer insert and open it up as flat as it will go.

4. Place the meat you want to smoke—chicken thighs or breasts, fish fillets, and small cuts of pork (i.e., not shoulders, but chops or loins or a rack or two of ribs) are best for this type of cooking—on top of the steamer. Note: You don't want to overcrowd the food on the steamer.

5. Close the pot with a lid. Seal the pot with foil all around the outside of the lid, tightly scrunching it up—you're trying to seal in the smoke and make sure it doesn't escape the pot.

6. Put the pot over high heat on the stove for about 5 minutes, or until the smoking gets started—some smoke will inevitably escape, so look for that, but if it doesn't and the pot has been on high for 5 minutes, it's safe to turn it down.

7. Lower the heat to medium low and cook 10 to 15 minutes for small cuts like chicken or fish, or 30 to 40 minutes for large pieces of meat (which might still need finishing in the oven, depending on weight and doneness).

8. Shut off the heat. Let the food rest in the smoker for about 20 minutes. Don't touch it, don't uncover it . . . don't even think about it. Let it rest and do its thing.

9. Remove the foil. If the meat is cooked through, it's ready to eat right now; if not, transfer it to a baking sheet and finish cooking it in the oven.

Q:

What kind of wood should I use? Do you use different woods for different types of food?

A:

People ask questions about what kind of wood to use all the time. I think it's because I make such a big deal of the fact that I use peach wood. I use peach wood, people, because I live in South Georgia, and Georgia is "the peach state." That's not me talking—that's literally the state's official nickname.

Here's the deal with wood: I like fruitwoods. Three reasons: They're mild in flavor, they have fewer impurities, and they have a natural sweetness to them. "Mild" here is a good thing when you're trying to build layers.

The wood is the base coat of flavor for your barbecue. It should have a subtle flavor that's not going to dominate the meat. The easiest thing you could possibly do is take advantage of the wood that's local, the wood that grows on the trees nearest to you. What grows near you? Apples are grown in thirty-two states, the top three of which are Washington, New York, and Michigan. Pears are grown in large quantities in California, Oregon, and Pennsylvania. You see what I mean? If you live only where hardwoods like hickory and oak are available, know that you can use those and they can make food taste great—but they should be combined with fruitwoods to mellow them out, otherwise your food will come out too harshly flavored. If you can't get your hands on some good local fruitwood, you can, of course, use other types and they'll work very well for you. Seven varieties of mesquite trees alone grow in the state of Texas.

What's the deal with the water pan, and do I have to use one?

I can't make you do anything, but if I could, it would be to use a water pan in your smoker when you cook barbecue. And you would thank me for it. Why? Because putting a pan of water in the bottom of your smoker helps the meat retain moisture during a cooking process that can otherwise dry it out. And keeping the meat moist throughout the cooking process means that when you eat it, it will be more tender. This is a no-brainer, folks: Fill a heavy-bottom medium-size pan, no bigger than a simple 13 by 9-inch lasagna pan, with water, then gently transfer it to the bottom of your smoker, right next to the hot coals and below where your meat will go. After you've finished cooking your meat, let your smoker cool down completely, remove your pan, clean it, and use it again. Even easier: You can just use aluminum baking pans filled with water if you like, and you can throw them away when you're done.

Note: Generally speaking, a water pan dries out somewhere between four and five hours into a cooking time—so if you're going to be smoking for more than that, plan to refill your water pan at that mark.

What ingredients should I keep stocked in my pantry?

One of the things that competition barbecue prepares you for is the need to be just that: prepared. You don't know in any given contest what kind of weather might crop up, or what you might've forgotten to pack or stock on your rig. Having a prestocked pantry of barbecue essentials at home is a tremendous luxury that I suggest you take full advantage of—set yourself up for success so that when you're ready to take on a project, you have everything you need. That begins with equipment and meat selection, but when it comes time for cooking and prep, these are the items that I find it best to have on hand. Note that unless I specify otherwise, I am not particular about what brand you buy; I have my favorites and I'm sure you have yours. Technique matters, and the quality of your meat matters. I've said this twice already but I'm going to say it a third time because it's that important: *If you start out with good-quality ingredients, your food will taste better.*

MYRON'S PANTRY ESSENTIALS

Sweeteners:

Light brown sugar

Dark brown sugar

Granulated sugar

Maple syrup

Light corn syrup

Honey

Condiments:

Ketchup

Mayonnaise

Worcestershire sauce

Yellow mustard

Vinegars:

Distilled white vinegar

Apple cider vinegar

Juices:

Apple juice

Lemon juice (have plenty of fresh lemons on hand, or buy imitation)

Pear nectar

Peach nectar

Jams and jellies:

Apple jelly

Blackberry preserves

Apricot preserves

Peach preserves

Broths:

Chicken broth

Beef broth concentrate (I like Minor's Original Formula Beef Base, which is widely available online)

Prepared pork stock (it's hard to find but great to have around if you can find it)

Spices:

Kosher salt

Fresh black peppercorns for grinding (nothing beats freshly ground black pepper in my book)

Accent Flavor Enhancer (also known as MSG, or mono-sodium glutamate, which I believe is a wonderful source of flavor; you can substitute a Cajun spice blend if you feel otherwise)

Garlic powder

Chili powder

Cumin

Onion powder

Paprika

Smoked salt (great for flavoring finished foods)*

A good classic barbecue spice rub*

A good spice rub for chicken*

A good spice rub for ribs*

Enhancers:

Imitation butter flavoring (this is for squirt bottles and spritzing; very useful)

A good classic barbecue sauce*

A good mustard-based barbecue sauce*

A good barbecue sauce for chicken*

A good vinegar-based barbecue sauce*

* Yes, I make my own line of sauces and rubs. Remember, that's how I got into the competitive barbecue world in the first place: I was just looking for a way to promote my family's sauce. (You're damn right I'm going to use this opportunity to try to sell them to you. You are always free to turn the page—or visit my online store at myronmixon.com and buy these excellent products . . . it's up to you.)

How do I keep my work station and prep area sanitary?

I used to get confused by this question, honestly. I was like: Is this whole world about to be taken over by folks who obsess over hand sanitizer? But it's not a stupid question, because barbecue involves handling raw meat—a lot of it, and fairly often. There are some basics rules of the trade that I always make sure to follow:

DO wash hands before and after prepping food, especially after handling raw meat and poultry.

DO keep your cooker clean. Germs can lurk on surfaces—so even if you let yours go unused for a little while, make sure to give it a good cleaning before you use it again.

DO use separate tools. Separate sets of tongs for handling raw meat and cooked meat, and utensils and cutting boards for raw meat and poultry to avoid cross contamination.

DO invest in a good food thermometer. Cooking food at the proper temperature is extremely important.

I've got a couple of other ways of handling hygiene. One, when I'm doing my prep I always wear disposable gloves made of nitrile rubber. These to me are the most sanitary, and they're both stronger than latex and more flexible, and good for folks who are allergic to latex, too. That's why a lot of folks in the food-service business prefer them, including me. They're easy to find—even I sell the heavy, thick black ones I like—and they're one form of insurance for sanitation. I also line all of my work tables and other work surfaces with plastic tablecloths before I start. It makes it so much easier to just roll up the mess and throw it out as soon as I'm finished. And finally, I use a lot of aluminum foil and aluminum pans. Why? They are the absolutely easiest and safest way to handle meat. For example, when you're transferring meat into the smoker, it never falls apart if you put it in a pan. And they sure make cleanup a lot easier. Another plus: If you cook in aluminum pans like I do, you don't have to scrape down your grill grates nearly as often.

"I was like: Is this whole world about to be taken over by folks who obsess over hand sanitizer?"

Q:

Is it actually important to rest the meat when it comes off the grill or smoker?

A:

It's so important that "actually important" doesn't even cover it. Resting your meat when it comes off the grill or out of the smoker is CRUCIAL. You need to let that meat rest, covered loosely with a "tent" of foil on a cutting board, for at least fifteen minutes and sometimes much, much longer (I'm thinking of a whole hog here), depending on the cut and the size. I give specific rest times for each meat recipe in this book, and that's for a reason: Resting the meat allows the meat's flavor to concentrate, its texture to solidify, and its temperature to evenly distribute throughout the cut. If you do not rest your meat properly and simply pull it off the grill or out of the smoker and cut into it, all the delicious juices and their delicious flavors are going to run right out of it—your cutting board will end up tasting better than your meat. But if you can find your patience and take care to rest your meat, the temperature has a chance to come down slightly, which means the meat's muscle fibers have a chance to relax, and when that happens it gives the juices and the wonderful flavors they carry with them a chance to settle and distribute themselves evenly throughout the meat. Do not, and I mean do not, skip the step of resting your meat, no matter how hungry you are or how hangry your guests might be getting. It's worth that extra few minutes. Suggestion: Have another drink, chill out, and boom, it'll be time to eat before you know it.

Q:

How should I start my fire?

A:

If you have ever watched even a minute or two of a barbecue cooking television show, you have inevitably heard the term "stick burner." It just means using real wood as fuel. It means starting off your smoking and barbecuing with wood first, not charcoals. And what is charcoal, after all, but the residue that you get from burning wood? What does this have to do with how to start a fire in your smoker? Everything.

Some folks have accused me of *not* being a stick burner because I actually start my fires with charcoal first, in order to get a blaze going that I then use to burn my wood—and thus create more charcoal, so I can start smoking my food over real wood smoke. That's just silly. I often start my fire with charcoal for ease. And I sometimes use lighter fluid to do it, which is even more controversial. Look, I don't have to prove anything to people: I know how to start a fire with a lightered knot, which is the way my daddy did it and the way I do it when I'm doing my pit barbecue class. If you don't know what that even means, Google it—it's about as old-school as you can get, apart from rubbing two sticks together and praying for a miracle. All I can tell you is this: People who say that using lighter fluid to start a fire will make your food taste like lighter fluid just ain't reading the directions for how to correctly use lighter fluid. Here's how I start my fires, and this is as foolproof as it gets, folks:

HOW TO START A FIRE THE MYRON WAY

Step One: If using lighter fluid, read the directions on the bottle; if you follow them, your food won't taste like lighter fluid.

Step Two: Fill your water pan if your smoker has one. Or place your water pan on the bottom of the smoker, next to where the charcoal will go.

Step Three: Start your fire in a charcoal chimney. I prefer briquettes to lump because they burn hotter and cleaner. If using, pour on the lighter fluid. Ignite the coals. When the coals ash over, transfer them into your smoker or grill. If you're using wood as your main fuel, the charcoal goes on top of it.

Step Four: If you're using coals as your main fuel, put your hardwood chips, which you've soaked overnight or at least several hours beforehand, directly on the hot coals so they'll smolder and provide smoke.

ESSENTIAL TOOLS TO HAVE ON HAND FOR SMOKING

— A charcoal chimney

— Plenty of hardwood briquettes or lump charcoal

— A couple of long-handled basting brushes (natural bristles won't melt like plastic bristles can; a mop-style baster is good to have, too)

— Plenty of disposable aluminum pans of varying sizes and depths

— A chef's knife, a paring knife, and a slicer

— Rib skimmer (such as the Myron Mixon Rib Skimmer)

— Long-handled tongs (at least two sets, one for raw foods and one for cooked foods; I like them spring-loaded)

— A reliable instant-read meat thermometer or two

— A reliable grill thermostat

— Food-grade gloves for handling raw meat

— Kitchen syringes/injectors

— Spray bottles/a mister for spritzing

— Heavy-duty oven mitts

— A small grill brush or grill scraper (for cleaning the grates)

CHAPTER THREE

PREPARE YOURSELF

MEAT PREP

Championship
St. Louis Ribs
page 189

What are the steps to building a flavor profile?

Marinades are the solutions that meats soak in to get additional flavor and moisture. They add zest and tang as well as help break down the meat's muscle fibers so that the meat tenderizes as it cooks.

Injections are simply marinades that you load into syringes and then apply into the center or other hard-to-reach places of dense or otherwise difficult-to-cook cuts of meat.

Rubs season the meat, help seal in moisture, and ensure that the meat develops a nice savory and browned crust (or "bark") on the outside.

Glazes are "finishing sauces" that, at the final stage of cooking, add a layer of caramelized flavor, thanks to their sugar, and add burnished color to the meat that you're smoking.

Sauces are what you pour on your meat or dip it into after it's finished cooking. They enhance the smoked flavors and textures of cooked meats, but are not technically a part of them.

> *Here's the deal:* Although I won't give you the formulas for the rubs, sauces, and marinades that I am creating for competitions this year, I will give you the recipes for the winning products I've made in years past. You can use these, adapt them, and develop your own successful blends.

Do I need to marinate my meat?

Marinades, of course, are the solutions you use to soak your meat in before you cook them. They flavor the meat, and they soften it. The time needed for successful marinating depends on the size of what you're planning to cook and also on the texture, which both help determine how quickly the solution can penetrate the center of the food. For example, if you have a very lean cut of meat that tends toward drying out, you need an oily marinade to infuse it with additional fat and flavor. An acidic marinade benefits an especially tough piece of meat because its acids break down and tenderize dense tendons and fibrous strands. If you marinate anything too long, though, you risk turning your meat mushy and losing something of its texture and its bite.

A good rule of thumb on marinades: Make them fresh right before you want to use them. Don't make them too far in advance or let them sit around in the refrigerator. You want them to be as fresh, flavorful, and concentrated as possible.

A word about injecting: A marinade can only penetrate into a piece of meat so much, and that's why some pitmasters like me also inject some of our larger cuts of meat with marinades, too. These injections are designed to help the marinade's flavors penetrate deep into the meat, and for that reason we load up large kitchen syringes and shoot the marinade right into the center of those tough cuts. When a judge does a site visit at a Memphis Barbecue Network event, he or she will want to taste the meat that's right next to the bone, deep on the inside of a cut. The fact is, a dry rub isn't ever going to be able to reach that area. That's why you need an injection. Some people ask me if marinades and injections are the same: Yes, they are. They're just applied differently, that's all.

Injecting is a good technique for dense pieces of meat like pork shoulder, brisket, and of course, whole hogs. The only tricky thing about injections is that you need to make sure the marinade you make doesn't contain anything that could clog up the syringe—you can't have any particles of herbs and spices in an injection the way you can in a traditional marinade, and you don't want the marinade itself to be too thick and viscous to get through the syringe if you're injecting it. In each individual recipe that follows this chapter, I've given very specific directions for where and how to inject the meats.

What follows are the formulas I like to use, and I want to encourage you to master them and then use them as blueprints for creating your own. I'm going to give you three of the most indispensable marinades (which can double as injections) that I have ever cooked up, and you take it from here.

"A good rule of thumb on marinades: Make them fresh right before you want to use them."

PORK MARINADE

It's very easy to multiply this recipe to make larger amounts for big pork shoulders. You'll need about 5 quarts for a whole hog, and 2 or 3 for a shoulder, depending on how large it is. You can store the marinade in your refrigerator for up to a year, but make sure you don't contaminate it, and always discard any used marinade—you can't keep it.

ingredients

3¼ cups apple juice

¼ cup distilled white vinegar

1 pound sugar

½ cup salt

¼ cup Accent Flavor Enhancer or a Cajun seasoning blend

In a large stockpot, combine the apple juice and vinegar over medium heat. Stirring continuously, pour in the sugar, salt, and seasoning. Keep stirring until the seasonings are completely dissolved, but do not let the mixture come to a boil. When all of the seasonings have dissolved, remove the pot from the heat. Let the liquid cool completely, then pour into a quart-size container. If not using this marinade/injection right away, you can store it in the refrigerator for up to six months. Make sure you shake it well before using.

BEEF MARINADE

This is tailor-made for your brisket, and the idea behind it is to infuse as much rich, beefy flavor into the beef as you can. It's simple and effective.

ingredients

1 quart water

3 tablespoons Minor's Original Formula Beef Base or other beef bouillon powder

1 15-ounce can strong beef broth

In a large stockpot over high heat, bring the water to a boil. Add the beef base and the broth and stir to dissolve. Do not bring to a boil. When dissolved, remove the pot from the heat. Allow the marinade to cool completely and pour into a quart-size container. This can be stored in the refrigerator for up to two weeks.

TANGY SWEET CHICKEN MARINADE

MAKES 1 QUART

Chicken does not need to be injected, in my opinion. But it definitely benefits from marinating, and I highly recommend this one.

ingredients

1 cup apple cider vinegar

¼ cup distilled white vinegar

1 cup vegetable oil

½ cup honey

½ cup soy sauce

¼ cup tomato paste

1 tablespoon garlic powder

1 tablespoon salt

1 teaspoon allspice

1 teaspoon white pepper

Combine all the ingredients in a heavy medium stockpot. Stir well to combine. Bring to a boil, cover, and reduce the heat to low. Simmer for 10 to 15 minutes. Let cool completely before using.

RIB MARINADE

MAKES 1 QUART

Don't listen to folks who say ribs don't need marinating. It's OK to listen to folks who do a dry marinade on ribs with a rub—people have a lot of success with that method—but I prefer to soak my ribs overnight in this wet marinade before I apply rub to them.

ingredients

½ liter ginger ale or ginger beer

2 cups orange juice

½ cup soy sauce

1 cup salt

1 (1-ounce) packet dry ranch-flavored salad-dressing mix

In a large bowl, combine all the ingredients. Stir well to thoroughly incorporate. Pour into a quart-size container and store, refrigerated, for up to 2 weeks. Shake well before using.

Do I need to use a rub?

I have a question for you: Do you know what a rub is? I've heard people talk about rubs as if they were run-of-the-mill seasonings, just like salt and pepper that you sprinkle onto your scrambled eggs, and that is just plain wrong. Rubs are a very specific thing, and they have a very specific job.

A rub is a dry mixture of spices, herbs, salt, and sugar that is applied to the surface of any protein you want to grill or smoke. A rub coats the food, and when it's applied properly it creates a crust around it that seals in both moisture and flavors. The rub is an important element in building the "flavor profile" you hear cooks talk so much about. It's a significant base layer that you need to have, period.

What makes a good rub: You have to have some salt, and you have to balance that with sugar. From there, the rest is pretty much wide open. You can try any combination of herbs and spices that you like and see what tastes good to you. That said, I do have a few rules of thumb for concocting rubs that will make your meat taste prize-winning:

Kosher salt/coarse ground salt: I like to use kosher salt (why "kosher"? see page 72) in all of my rubs. The reason is that this course-grained salt has a larger grain size than typical table salt, and is not iodized like table salt is. Iodine lends a funny flavor that you don't need in your smoked foods. There's also an issue of texture: Smaller salt crystals like the kind you find in table salt dissolve quickly—almost instantly, really—which makes oversalting food a lot easier to do because you can't see how much salt is on it. Not only can you see kosher salt better because it doesn't dissolve as easily or as quickly, but it's also more pinch-able and has an easier-to-control texture—you pinch some table salt and those crystals are so tiny that you're likely to get twice as much salt as you need without even realizing it.

Sugar: I call for different types in different rubs. For example, I like to use brown sugar in some of my combinations, because I like the way it binds the other ingredients in the rub. It also provides increased caramelization on the surface of the meat. Other rubs I create use coarse sugar, which has a chunkier and crunchier texture and so tends to clump less. Also, because it contains natural molasses, it tends to brown evenly as well. For other recipes, regular white granulated sugar will work just fine.

For my meats, I like to have a flavorful red spice in the rub because it enhances the color of the meat's crust (in addition to flavoring it, of course). That's why you'll find ingredients like smoked and also sweet paprika, chipotle pepper powder, chili powder, and sometimes a dash or two of cayenne pepper in my rubs. That's something to keep in mind for presentation and visual effect.

3 cups: A good-size batch of rub for a couple of smoking projects is about 3 cups. Make that amount, and you're good for either a barbecue contest or a month of summertime smoking.

My final rule on rubs is: If you change your meats, change your rubs. Some rubs can be used on every kind of food you want to smoke—chicken, spareribs, salmon, brisket—but I believe that tweaking your rub recipe to accommodate for the natural flavors of your protein is a good idea. I'm going to give you a basic rub recipe, but I'm also going to show you that a chicken rub, for example, needs to be lighter in color and heavier on the garlic than, say, a rub I'd use on red meat or a whole hog. And I like brown sugar in my hog rubs because it ensures that the skin gets extra caramelized—and remember that there's a lot of hog skin to contend with, so you want it to turn out as golden brown and delicious as possible—as opposed to a brisket, which doesn't have any skin and thus doesn't need the same type of seasoning to develop a good crust. So is there a one-size-fits-all rub? Yes, there can be, but I encourage you to develop a profile of different rubs for your different proteins, as each one of these meats has its own personality and its own built-in flavor.

MEAT RUB

This rub is a good basic rub for almost any food you want to smoke. You can use it as a jumping-off point or a template, and then once you've mastered it, you can use the basic formula to create your own rubs.

ingredients

1 cup sugar

2 tablespoons chili powder

2 tablespoons mustard powder

2 tablespoons onion powder

2 tablespoons garlic powder

2 tablespoons ground cumin

½ teaspoon cayenne pepper

2 tablespoons kosher salt

2 tablespoons coarsely ground black pepper

In a large bowl, combine all the ingredients. Stir to combine thoroughly. You can store this rub in an airtight container indefinitely, but it'll begin to lose its strength after about 3 months—and if I had any left after 6 months, I'd make a new batch.

WHAT IS KOSHER SALT?

Is it actually kosher, as in blessed by a rabbi? Look, any salt can be certified as "kosher" if it is made under conditions approved by qualified rabbinical supervision. So the answer is that "kosher salt" can be kosher, and sometimes it is, but it's not always, and it doesn't have to be. Coarse-grain salt is referred to as "kosher salt" because the large size of its crystal grains is ideal for drawing out moisture from meat, which is essential for the koshering process of removing, or drawing out, the blood from meat.

CHICKEN RUB

ingredients

1 cup chili powder

1 cup sugar

3 tablespoons kosher salt

3 tablespoons onion powder

3 tablespoons garlic powder

3 tablespoons sweet
Hungarian paprika

1 teaspoon cayenne pepper

In a large bowl, combine all the ingredients. Stir to combine thoroughly. You can store this rub in an airtight container indefinitely, but it'll begin to lose strength after about 3 months— and if I had any left after 6 months, I'd make a new batch.

"If you change your meats, change your rubs. Some rubs can be used on every kind of food you want to smoke–chicken, spareribs, salmon, brisket–but I believe that tweaking your rub recipe to accommodate for the natural flavors of your protein is a good idea."

Q:

What is a "glaze,"
why do you use them, and
when do I need one?

A:

Because glazes contain sugar, they are great for caramelizing the crusts and surfaces of meats that are almost fully cooked. I like them a lot, not only because they add a layer of flavor to your meats but also because they help lock in a moist and tender texture. Glazing should always happen at the very end of cooking time. I give you specific information in each recipe on how to use these glazes to get in one last lick of flavor during the meat's cooking time and to get some good color on your meat before you take it out of the smoker. There are only two glazes you really need to master: one for chicken, and one for pork.

CHICKEN GLAZE

MAKES 3 CUPS

This is just what you need for your cupcake chicken (page 96), your chicken thighs, or if you want to get fancy and glaze a whole bird.

ingredients

½ cup ketchup

½ cup Jack's Old South Vinegar Sauce or make your own (see page 78)

½ cup Jack's Old South Hickory Sauce or make your own (see page 77)

½ cup honey

½ cup maple syrup

½ cup dark brown sugar

4 tablespoons (½ stick) unsalted butter, melted

Pour all the ingredients into the base of a large blender. Blend thoroughly to combine for about 3 minutes. Pour the mixture into a medium pot and, over medium heat, stir constantly until the sauce is hot. Do not allow it to come to a boil. Remove from the stove and glaze your chicken while the sauce is still warm.

If you are reserving this for a later use, pour the sauce into a large container. Store, refrigerated, for up to 2 months. Always reheat this glaze before using.

PORK GLAZE

MAKES 3½ CUPS

If you're making a whole hog, you need to triple this recipe. For a shoulder, depending on how large it is—a whole shoulder versus a butt, for example—you may need to double it. For pork chops or a pork loin, this alone will do you right, and you may even have some left over.

ingredients

1 cup Jack's Old South Vinegar Sauce or make your own (see page 78)

1½ cups apple jelly

1 cup light corn syrup

Pour all the ingredients into the base of a large blender. Blend thoroughly to combine for about 3 minutes. Transfer to a bowl, using a spatula to scrape all of the glaze out of the blender. Store covered in the refrigerator for up to 2 weeks.

Which barbecue sauce do you like best?

Good lord, the kinds of questions I get about sauces. It's as if some folks out there think the sauce makes the barbecue. Here's the deal: You cannot make bad barbecue taste good with a sauce. There ain't no sauce in the world—except maybe my own, and even then I wouldn't bet on it—that can make mediocre barbecue taste delicious. What a sauce *can* do is add an excellent complementary or perfectly contrasting note to barbecue that is already good. It can take great barbecue into the next stratosphere, and that is why you should bother with it.

It's not that I think sauces aren't important: What I think is that sauces are given an exaggerated importance for novice cooks, and that if you learn to smoke properly, you won't have to be so worried about your sauces in the first place. Sauces are the last step in a process of flavoring smoked meats, and their main job is to *enhance*. They are helpers. A sauce is not the star of the show, or at least it shouldn't be—if you're telling me the best thing about a cook's barbecue is his sauce, I'm thinking that the cook in question probably can't cook.

As you also already know, the world is full of sauces—just look in the aisles of your grocery store. Sauces can be made out of every damn ingredient you have in your refrigerator or pantry, from sour cream to cola to blueberry pie filling. And just as different areas of our country have different ways of cooking barbecue—see page 27, where I go into the most prevalent styles—they also favor different types of sauces. That's cool, but I'm based in South Georgia and I favor vinegar-based sauces. But I know how to make several other varieties that I'll share with you (for example, my momma's family's mustard-based sauce, page 79).

BARBECUE SAUCE

This is the kind of sauce that most people have in their minds when they think of barbecue sauce—it's a down-the-middle, universal variety that approximates the sweet and strong woodsy flavor of hickory. It's very good on beef, pork, or lamb.

ingredients

2 tablespoons onion powder

2 tablespoons garlic powder

2 cups ketchup

2 tablespoons paprika

⅔ cup apple cider vinegar

2 tablespoons Worcestershire sauce

¼ cup dark brown sugar

2 tablespoons honey

2 tablespoons maple syrup

2 tablespoons kosher salt

2 tablespoons freshly ground black pepper

Combine all the ingredients in the base of a blender; pulse until thoroughly combined. Pour into a medium pot. Over medium heat, stir continuously until the sauce is heated through. Do not allow it to boil. Remove from the heat and use the sauce immediately, while hot.

If reserving for a later use, allow the mixture to cool, then pour it into a large bottle or container. Store in the refrigerator for up to six months.

"There ain't no sauce in the world—except maybe my own, and even then I wouldn't bet on it—that can make mediocre barbecue taste delicious."

VINEGAR-BASED BARBECUE SAUCE

MAKES 3½ CUPS

This sauce is peppery and piquant and I like to use it on any old food—but it really sings on pork shoulder and whole hog. It is thin and spicy with a hint of sweetness, and it's addictive.

ingredients

2 cups apple cider vinegar

1 cup ketchup

½ cup hot sauce

2 tablespoons kosher salt

2 tablespoons freshly ground black pepper

1 tablespoon crushed red pepper flakes

½ cup sugar

In a stockpot over medium heat, combine the vinegar, ketchup, and hot sauce. Stir to combine. Add in the spices and sugar and stir to dissolve. Stir continuously until the sauce is heated through. Do not allow it to boil. When the spices are thoroughly dissolved, take the pot off the heat. Allow the sauce to cool completely. Pour the sauce into a large bottle or container. Store in the refrigerator for up to six months.

TANGY SWEET SAUCE

MAKES 3½ CUPS

This sauce is designed for lighter-flavored meats like chicken and turkey, and it's dynamite on them. You could use it on shrimp and seafood as well.

ingredients

1 cup apple cider vinegar

½ cup ketchup

¼ cup hot sauce

1 tablespoon kosher salt

1 tablespoon freshly ground black pepper

2 teaspoons crushed red pepper flakes

1 cup light corn syrup

1 cup peach preserves

In a stockpot over medium heat, combine the vinegar, ketchup, and hot sauce. Stir to combine. Pour in the spices and stir to dissolve. Over medium heat, stir continuously until the sauce is heated through. Do not allow it to boil. When the spices are thoroughly dissolved, take the pot off the heat. Allow the mixture to cool completely. Once it has cooled, pour into the base of a blender along with the corn syrup and the peach preserves. Blend until thoroughly combined. The sauce will be on the thick side. Pour into a large container or bottle. Store in the refrigerator for up to six months.

CAROLINA MUSTARD BARBECUE SAUCE

South Carolinians in particular are known for their love of mustard-based barbecue sauce, which they slather all over their pork. It's got a hint of sweetness to it and a big hit of vinegar. Some North Carolinians who take pride in their vinegar-based sauce, which I also love, look down their noses at mustard sauces. It don't matter to me as long as it tastes good, and this sauce is very, very good on pulled pork and chicken.

ingredients

2 cups white vinegar

2 teaspoons freshly ground black pepper

2 teaspoons white sugar

2 teaspoons crushed red pepper flakes

2 teaspoons ground chili powder

1 cup dark brown sugar, packed

2½ cups prepared yellow mustard

¼ cup ketchup

In a large heavy saucepan or stockpot over low heat add all the ingredients and whisk to combine. Cook over low heat for 20 minutes, whisking occasionally to combine. Do not bring the mixture to a boil. Let the sauce cool completely, about 30 minutes, then funnel it into a refrigerator-safe container. The sauce will keep, refrigerated, for up to a year.

CHAPTER FOUR

YARDBIRDS, DEMYSTIFIED

CHICKEN & TURKEY

Smoked Turkey
page 126

Classic Creamy
Coleslaw
page 297

Peach
Baked Beans
page 301

Smoked
Half Chickens
page 107

Smoky
Collard Greens
page 303

CHICKEN CUTS

TURKEY CUTS

What kind of chickens and turkeys should I buy?

You can buy whatever type of chicken and turkey you like, of course, but believe me when I tell you that it makes a difference when it comes to taste. In all my years of cooking and eating chickens and turkeys, I've come to realize that how these birds are raised has a big impact on how they taste, and not all birds are raised the same. A lot has changed about poultry and livestock farming during my lifetime. When I was growing up, it was fine to go to your local grocery and buy any old bird—in a small town in the South, you knew the grocer as well as the farm where the chicken was raised and slaughtered. But we all know that's not so common anymore. The closest I'm able to come to that kind of standard is to buy birds that are certified organic with no added antibiotics or growth hormones. There are plenty of good options for chicken and turkey in almost every supermarket now. If you can get one from a local farmer who you know or who's at your nearby farmers' market, so much the better. No matter where you buy it, look for the freshest birds that are naturally raised without antibiotics and preferably fed organic feed. Just know that the extra few dollars will be worth it in your end product.

About the size of the chickens: Of course whole chicken sizes vary—I've seen small birds that are barely over a pound and others that run up to four or more. I tend to like smaller birds because they smoke faster; but whatever size chicken you buy, keep in mind the weight of that chicken when you're calculating how long it'll need to be in the smoker. If you're buying multiple chickens and plan to cook them at the same time, aim for all of them to be about the same size.

What's best to barbecue: a whole chicken or cut-up chicken pieces?

The "pieces versus whole bird" question is strictly a matter of personal preference. For instance, when you smoke a whole bird you're just dealing with one thing, one large "piece," if you will, so it's easy to manage from that standpoint. However, it takes longer to cook a whole bird than it does to cook a collection of its parts, and you have to grapple with the fact that the pieces don't all get done at the same time. If you're doing pieces, it takes less time and once you get each leg or wing or breast done to your individual specifications, all you gotta do is rest it until the other pieces are ready, then bring it to the table and eat it. I do understand that for some occasions people like the presentation of the whole bird rather than a platter of pieces, but to my mind it doesn't matter either way—and cooking pieces is easier, if that makes a difference to you.

When it comes to chickens in particular, note that there are trends to how they're cut up in groceries and butcher shops. Nowadays the standard is for chickens to be cut up into eight pieces: two legs, two thighs, two breasts, and two wings. When I was growing up, though, most butchers cut chickens into eleven pieces: two legs, two thighs, two breasts, two wings, and also the neck, back, and wishbone. Neck, back, and wishbone are used for other purposes today by butchers and groceries, and home cooks today don't seem to have much value for these "spare parts." Because I grew up having those additional pieces around to enjoy, I like to smoke them when I cook chicken. And even though you can buy a cut-up chicken in any grocery store in America, buying one already cut up is always more expensive. That's why I'm going to tell you how to cut up a chicken yourself—into eight or eleven parts, your choice. With that knowledge, you're free to buy the freshest chicken you can from any farmer or meat market and butcher it yourself, like I do.

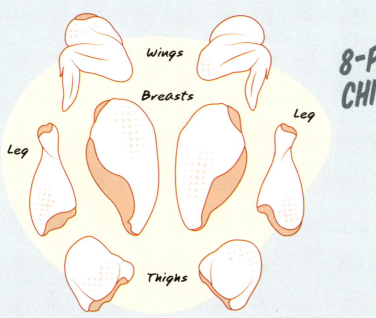

8-PIECE CHICKEN

Wings

Breasts

Leg

Leg

Thighs

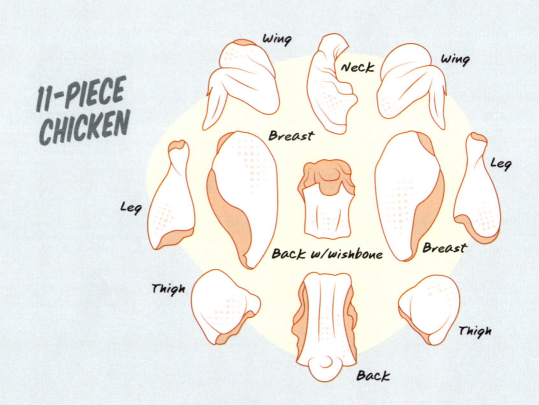

11-PIECE CHICKEN

Wing

Neck

Wing

Breast

Leg

Leg

Back w/wishbone

Breast

Thigh

Thigh

Back

HOW TO CUT UP A CHICKEN

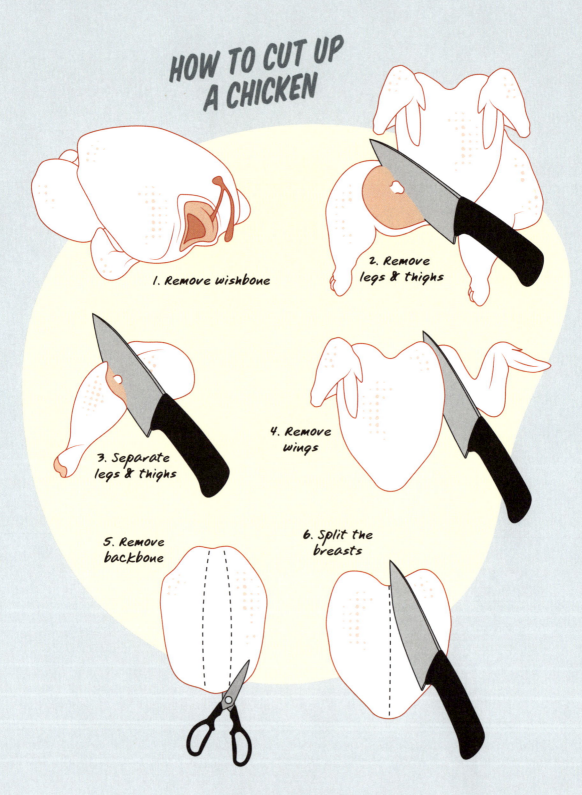

1. Remove wishbone

2. Remove legs & thighs

3. Separate legs & thighs

4. Remove wings

5. Remove backbone

6. Split the breasts

How should I prep my chicken?

I have a standard meat prep that I do on all the meat I smoke, but if I'm planning to butcher a chicken I wait until I've cut the bird into pieces first. Then I put it on a cutting board that's designated for raw meat, breast facing up.

Before you get started, make sure to remove the giblets and neck from the inside of the chicken. You can set them aside or freeze them so you can roast them and make stock with them, or you can smoke the necks. Or simply discard the necks and giblets immediately if you can't find a use for them. I always laugh when people talk about being "nose to tail" meat users: Poor people in the South ate every bit of every animal long before it was fashionable to do that.

Now to the bird: Run the blade of a large sharp kitchen knife along the shoulder (the cavity where the neck was removed) to expose the wishbone. Once you've located the wishbone, use the blade to cut through the cartilage around the wishbone, loosening it equally on both sides. Use your fingers to further separate the wishbone from the breasts, feeling your way to the top where the wishbone connects to the breastbone. Then grab the top of that wishbone, give it a good twist-and-pull, and cleanly detach it. Set it aside if you want to clean it and then pull it for luck; otherwise, discard it.

Next: Using your hands, gently pull the legs away from the body to loosen and dislodge them a bit from their joints. Using your sharp knife, cut through the connective skin and tissue on one side until you reach the leg bone. Hopefully you'll hit the joint where the thigh meets the body, but if you don't, simply use the tip of your knife to locate it. Once the joint is reached, press the knife through it, cutting through the cartilage and separating the thigh and leg from the body of the bird. Take the separate leg and thigh: Use your fingers to feel where the thighbone meets the drumstick. There will be a vertical line of fat that you'll be able to see—the joint is right beneath it. Use your knife to cut through the connecting joint, separating the thigh from the leg. Now repeat the process on the other side: See where you started the thigh and leg cutting on the first side, and then find the same area on the leg and thigh that are still attached. Once again, use your knife to cut straight down through the connective skin and tissue until you reach the joint attaching the thigh to the body. As before, once the joint is reached, just press the knife through it and separate the thigh and leg from the body of the bird. After the thigh and leg are removed, separate them at the joint the way you did with the other side.

Now the body of the bird has only the breast and wing attached. First, you want to separate the wings: Use your thumb to feel along the wing for the joint that connects it to the breast; you should feel a little ridge. Lift up the wing and shake it gently to loosen and dislodge it, then cut along that ridge to separate it from the breast. Do the same on the opposite side to remove the other wing.

The second-to-last step is to remove the backbone. A lot of people find that using kitchen shears makes this part easier because you'll be cutting through bone—but you can stick with your knife if it's sharp enough. The first step is to rotate the carcass so that it's breast side down on the cutting board. Now find your backbone: Once again, there are lines of fat to look for on either side that separate the backbone from the breast. Once you find those, simply use your knife or shears and cut down, through the ribs, about three-quarters of the length of the bird. Once you've cut about three-quarters of the way down along the backbone of the bird on both sides, you can use your hands to gently but firmly bend the backbone back and pull it apart from the breast. Most folks do some combination of breaking and cutting to get the backbone off. (You can throw that backbone into a stockpot immediately, or roast it and then make stock out of it, freeze it and save it to make stock later, or simply discard it.)

Finally, you've got your whole bone-in breasts, still attached. If you're going to smoke this bird, you should leave the breasts attached to the bones, but you still need to separate them. To do that, place the breasts on the cutting board with the bone side up. Use your sharp knife to cut all the way down the bone that connects them; your goal is to break the bone but not to cut all the way through the breasts and separate them yet. After you've cut along that bone, flip the breasts up on the cutting board. Press down on the center of the breasts to flatten them out, and use your fingers to smooth the skin down on both sides. Now use your knife to cut through the breasts; you'll have to go just halfway because you've already made one cut on the bottom side. Now you have two big breasts, which you can further cut in half if you want smaller pieces (I don't, but some people prefer that). And now you've got your cut-up chicken, and a bonus pot of stock.

"I always laugh when people talk about being 'nose to tail' meat users: Poor people in the South ate every bit of every animal long before it was fashionable to do that."

Do you have a good stock recipe?

I know, I know: All this cutting up of birds begs the question. Yes, I do. I prefer to make smoked stock because it's the most flavorful—I love to get that smoky flavor in my sauces, casseroles, stuffings, and side dishes, too. If you've just cut up a chicken, you can wrap its neck bone and backbone in aluminum foil and throw them in a small pan on the smoker, leave the pan in the smoker as long as it takes to cook your bird, and then use those smoked bones to make the most delicious stock you ever tasted.

SMOKED STOCK

This recipe will be the same no matter which bird you've smoked: turkey or chicken.

ingredients

1 carcass from a large smoked turkey or chicken

8 cloves garlic, peeled and smashed

3 large stalks celery, cleaned, dried, and roughly chopped

1 large sweet onion, peeled, trimmed and quartered

3 large carrots, cleaned, peeled, and roughly chopped

1 bay leaf

1 tablespoon Worcestershire sauce

Kosher salt, to taste

Freshly ground black pepper, to taste

In a large heavy Dutch oven or stockpot, combine all the ingredients. Cover with enough cold water to submerge all the ingredients, about 3 quarts. Over moderately high heat, bring the stock to a boil. Reduce the heat to low to let the stock simmer gently for at least 3 hours and not more than 4, periodically using a slotted spoon to skim the surface and discard the fat that collects on the surface. Remove the stock from the heat, cover the pot, and allow the stock to cool completely. Discard the bones and vegetables. Line a fine-mesh strainer or colander with several layers of cheesecloth. Place it over a large bowl.

You may need to strain it two or three times to remove all the solids. Refrigerate the stock overnight. The next day, the stock should be golden in color. Skim any fat that collects on the surface and discard the solids. After skimming, use immediately or pour it into containers to store. Store the stock in the refrigerator for five days, or in the freezer for about three months. Make sure to discard any fat that accumulates on top of the stock before using.

Do you still make "cupcake chicken"?

People ask me about "cupcake chicken" every single day of my life. It's amazing to me that something that once caused me so much vexation, which was cooking chicken in barbecue competitions, has become something that I'm now well-known for—it's pretty damn cool.

If you have never heard the cupcake chicken story before, or even if you have but you just like it a lot (as apparently many of you do, judging by the posts on my social media accounts and by the shout-outs I get at contests), let me tell you about my now world-famous cupcake chicken.

When it came to chicken, I spent years wandering in the proverbial desert at barbecue competitions. Chicken has always been the toughest damn category to cook in any contest. That's because judges expect all the pieces to be the same size and the same thickness, and getting chicken pieces to be that way takes a lot of prep time—it is tedious, exacting work. To give you an example, I can prep a whole hog in less time than it takes to prep chicken—and that's no exaggeration. My difficulty laid in figuring out how to get my chicken to taste delicious *and also* look perfect, at the same time. Most barbecue-contest competitors cook thighs because of all the chicken pieces, thighs are the easiest to uniformly size and trim. But they're still not *that* easy to deal with, believe me. So after losing in the chicken category every time—and y'all know how much I hate to lose—I put my thinking cap on: How could I make sure that my thighs were the same size, every time? Maybe I could try some type of mold, I thought. So I bought one of those silicon cupcake-muffin molds from the baking aisle in Walmart. But I realized that I would have to do something about the sauce and the draining of the liquid, so I came up with a way of nesting two pans while also allowing the bottom of the cups to drain. Then I butchered my chicken thighs, trying to get them as identically shaped and sized as possible. When I tried out my new method, smoked those thighs, and unmolded them, they looked like clones. Problem solved. And I started not only placing in the chicken category but also winning it.

But I still haven't answered the question. Yes, I do still make cupcake chicken—because if it ain't broke, don't fix it. What I do tinker with, and what I have changed over the years, is the seasonings and glazes and other flavor profiles of the chicken thighs in those muffin cups. That's how the world of competitive barbecue works: To succeed, you simply cannot keep cooking the same food in the same way every time at every contest. Barbecue is an evolving art, and even though pitmasters like me still rely on the ancient technique of smoking meat over fire, we still have to evolve with the times. Because too many other people are taking the time and spending the money to improve their barbecue—whether they invest in new equipment or in cooking classes or spend a lot of time in online forums swapping recipes and techniques—if you don't keep up, you'll be shut out in contests. You know what, though? I started making cupcake chicken ten years ago, and today I see many teams unpacking their muffin tins before they start smoking chicken—I have to laugh. If only you could patent a cooking technique, cupcake chicken would be funding my children's retirements.

The good news for you home cooks is that you don't have to worry about all your chicken pieces being the same size. But you can still use the muffin-tin method in your backyard—it makes it easy to make good-looking smoked and glazed chicken thighs that will wow and delight your friends and neighbors. Here is how I'm making cupcake chicken these days:

"Barbecue is an evolving art, and even though pitmasters like me still rely on the ancient technique of smoking meat over fire, we still have to evolve with the times."

CUPCAKE CHICKEN

MAKES 12 APPETIZER OR 6 MAIN COURSE SERVINGS

When I make cupcake chicken for competitions, we have to use bone-in chicken thighs. If you're cooking in your backyard, you can surely use the boneless thighs—it will save you a lot of time and aggravation.

ingredients

12 medium skin-on boneless chicken thighs

Apple cider vinegar

1 cup Jack's Old South Huney Muney Cluck Rub or make your own (see page 73)

3½ cups chicken broth

1 cup Jack's Old South Vinegar Sauce or make your own (see page 78)

2 cups Jack's Old South Hickory Sauce or make your own (see page 77)

½ cup tomato paste

½ cup honey

½ cup maple syrup

¾ cup seedless blackberry preserves

4 tablespoons (½ stick) unsalted butter, softened

tools

silicone cupcake mold, with holes punched through the bottom of each cup

13 by 9-inch aluminum baking pan

large aluminum baking sheet

Preheat a smoker to 300°F.

Use poultry shears or a sharp paring knife to trim any excess fat off the skin and meat of each thigh. Rub the thighs all over with apple cider vinegar, and then apply the rub evenly on both sides of each thigh. Place each thigh into one cup of the prepared mold. Set the mold inside the baking pan, then pour the broth into the bottom of the pan, taking care not to pour the broth directly on top of the chicken. Place the pan in the smoker, uncovered, and smoke for 1½ hours.

While thighs are smoking, make the sauce. In a blender, combine the two barbecue sauces, the tomato paste, honey, maple syrup, blackberry preserves, and butter. Blend until thoroughly combined. Transfer the sauce into a large saucepan. Over moderate heat, warm the sauce until it is hot but not boiling, stirring continuously. When the sauce has thoroughly combined and is warm throughout, remove from the burner and set aside to cool.

Remove the pan from the smoker. Carefully unmold the chicken thighs onto a clean aluminum baking sheet, skin side up. Brush the thighs lightly with the warm sauce. Place the baking sheet in the smoker and smoke for 30 minutes to allow the sauce to caramelize into the chicken skin.

Remove the thighs from the smoker. Let the thighs rest, loosely covered, for 30 minutes before serving.

*Why doesn't my rub stick
to my chicken?*

If your rub isn't sticking to your chicken, it's probably because you're taking the chicken out of its packaging or unwrapping it from plastic wrap and trying to apply the rub directly onto it without treating the meat first. What you need to try is rubbing it with white vinegar and patting it down thoroughly with paper towels or a clean kitchen towel. Now apply your rub and see if stays on your meat. Trust me, it will.

Q:

What's the secret to great barbecued chicken?

A:

This is a more complicated question than it might seem. Everybody loves barbecuing chicken. But exactly what they mean by "barbecued chicken" could be one of two distinctly different things. I'm going to break it down for you here, with definitions and recipes to go with both ideas of "barbecued chicken." (You can see page 25 for the difference between smoking and barbecuing if you want more information on this subject.)

BARBECUE CHICKEN #1

This is for people who are not actually talking about "barbecued" chicken. They're *not* talking about a whole chicken or chicken pieces that are smoked over wood fire at a low temperature in order to acquire a distinctly smoky essence. They're talking about a whole chicken that's been basted with barbecue sauce and then grilled over a high temperature to sear in juices and flavors. Here is a very easy to way to make a delicious version of this kind of "barbecued chicken."

The single best way to grill a whole chicken is to make it as evenly flat as possible. "Spatchcocking" is a cool old-fashioned term for butterflying the bird. This lets you flatten out the bird for more even, consistent cooking of the breast and legs together and allows you to do the kind of quick-cooking that grilling demands.

HOW TO BUTTERFLY A CHICKEN

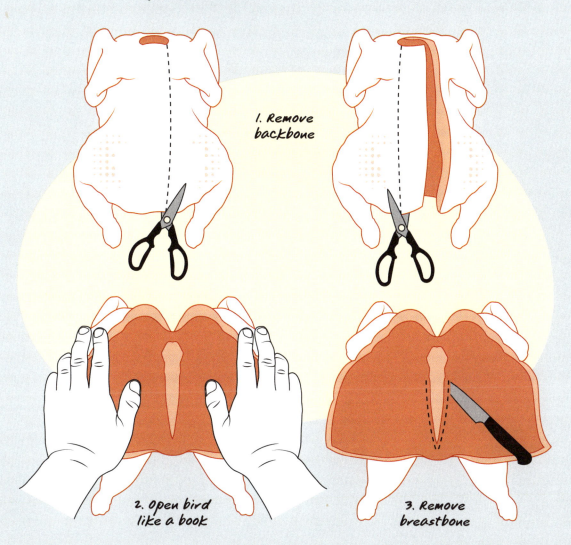

1. Remove backbone

2. Open bird like a book

3. Remove breastbone

WHOLE GRILLED BARBECUE CHICKEN

Good grilled chicken should have crisp, crackly, blistered skin all over its entire surface, with no soft spots or pockets of rubbery fat.

ingredients

1 (3½- to 4-pound) large whole chicken

½ cup apple cider vinegar

Kosher salt, to taste

Freshly ground black pepper, to taste

2 cups Jack's Old South Huney Muney Cluck Rub or make your own (see page 73)

To butterfly it: Get a sharp paring knife and a pair of kitchen shears. Place the chicken on a cutting board breast side down. Working from the cavity opening up to the neck, cut along each side of the backbone with the kitchen shears. Discard the backbone or reserve it for stock (page 93). Grab the chicken with one breast in each hand and open it like a book, exposing the cavity of the bird—you'll hear a crack, most likely. Running from the middle of the bird down between the two legs is the so-called "soft bone" or "keel bone"—this is the breastbone. It's a triangular shape that is firm toward the middle of the bird but becomes soft flexible cartilage as it tapers down between the legs. To remove it, use a paring knife to cut down either side of it. Once you've cut it free, use your fingers to loosen and then pull out the breastbone. Discard the bone, and your chicken is good to go.

Rub the chicken all over with the vinegar, then season it on both sides with salt and pepper. Generously smear the rub under and over the skin and on the interior of the bird. Place in a baking pan, cover with plastic wrap, and refrigerate at least three hours or preferably overnight.

When you are ready to cook the chicken, preheat half the grill to medium-high (or build a medium-high-heat fire on one side of a charcoal grill); leave the other half unheated.

Place the chicken skin side down over the heated side and grill until the skin begins to color and char marks form, about 5 minutes. Flip over and grill 5 minutes more. Move the chicken to the unheated side. Close the lid and cook, making sure the chicken is flat against the grate, skin side up, until an instant-read thermometer inserted into the thickest part of a thigh without touching bone registers 180°F, approximately 30 to 40 minutes. Transfer to a platter and let rest for 5 to 10 minutes before carving.

GRILLED BARBECUE CHICKEN THIGHS & LEGS

SERVES 6 TO 8

Let's say you don't want to bother with a whole chicken. Or let's say you're me, and you're just a person who happens to love the inexpensive versatility of chicken thighs and legs—you can cook them just about any old way, and because they're the fattiest parts of the bird, they have the most flavor. That's a win-win in my book. This is such an easy recipe—three ingredients, folks—that I recommend it to people when they ask me what they should make for dinner on a busy weeknight. It's not exactly "barbecuing" because you're not cooking meat over a low heat and infusing it with smoke, but it has a similar flavor profile and it makes for some really good eating. Note that I prefer bone-in thighs, but you can use boneless just as well if you like.

ingredients

8 whole chicken legs, split, or 8 drumsticks and 8 bone-in (or boneless) chicken thighs

½ cup white vinegar

1 cup Jack's Old South Huney Muney Cluck Rub or make your own (see page 73)

2 cups Jack's Old South Tangy Sweet Sauce or make your own (see page 78; optional)

Set up your charcoal or gas grill for indirect heat: Build a fire in your grill, leaving one side free of coals. When the coals are covered with gray ash and the temperature is medium-high (you can hold your hand 5 inches above the coals for about 5 seconds), you are ready to cook. (For a gas grill, turn one of the burners down to low or off, cover, and heat for 15 minutes.)

Wash the chicken pieces thoroughly in cold water, then dry them with paper towels or a clean kitchen towel. Rub the pieces all over with the vinegar. Apply the rub all over the exposed areas of the chicken pieces.

Arrange the chicken on the hot grate above the drip pan in your cooker and away from the coals or burner, skin side down. Cover and grill for about 40 minutes, opening the grill once about halfway through the cooking time to flip the pieces and covering the cooker again, until the skin is crisp, the meat is cooked through, and the thigh meat registers 180°F on an instant-read thermometer. Transfer to plates and serve immediately with the sauce on the side for dipping, if you like.

GRILLED BARBECUE CHICKEN BREASTS

SERVES 4

Because I know so many of us eat chicken breasts with great regularity these days, I'm going to tell you how you make them into "good barbecue." You didn't come to me to tell you how to grill a boneless, skinless breast, because you can figure that out yourself. What I can tell you is how to make a good quick barbecue-style chicken breast, for which you'll need to cook breasts that are still on the bone and have some skin attached. These breasts hold up much better for this type of hot and fast cooking without drying out like those boneless, skinless ones tend to do.

ingredients

4 chicken breast halves on the bone with skin (about 2 to 2½ pounds total)

¼ cup apple cider vinegar

3 cups Smoked Stock (page 93) or good-quality store-bought stock

1 cup Jack's Old South Huney Muney Cluck Rub or make your own (see page 73)

1 cup Jack's Old South Tangy Sweet Sauce, for serving (optional)

Rub them all over with the vinegar. Place the chicken breasts in one or more gallon-size zip-top bags and pour the stock over them. Seal the bag(s) and refrigerate for at least 3 hours, or preferably overnight.

When you are ready to cook, set up your charcoal or gas grill for indirect heat: Build a fire in your grill, leaving one side free of coals. When the coals are covered with gray ash and the temperature is medium-high (you can hold your hand 5 inches above the coals for about 5 seconds), you are ready to cook. (For a gas grill, turn one of the burners down to low or off, lower the cover, and heat for 15 minutes.)

Remove the chicken from the marinade. Pat dry all over. Coat liberally on both sides with the rub. Place the chicken breasts on the grill skin side up. Cover and grill the chicken until browned and just cooked through, about 30 minutes. Turn the breasts over and grill until the skin is crisp and lightly charred, about 2 to 5 minutes more. Transfer the breasts to a cutting board and let them rest, loosely covered with foil, for 5 minutes. Serve with the sauce on the side for dipping, if you like.

BARBECUE CHICKEN #2

Now we're going to talk about doing some actual barbecue cooking, by which I mean smoking. There are a couple of different ways to smoke a chicken, and I'm going to give you my two favorites. The first is for a simple way to smoke a whole bird, and then I'll give you a method my dad, Jack, loved, which was smoking chicken halves. Those are easy and fun to serve, too.

ALL ABOUT BRINING

One thing I do with my barbecue that my daddy didn't is brine my whole birds. The white meat really benefits from some additional flavor, that's why: We need some salt in there, to pull some flavor in, and that's key to any brining process.

To brine a whole bird: In a large stockpot, combine **3 gallons water**, **3 cups kosher salt**, and **3 cups white sugar**. (If you want to add some other ingredients in there, favorite herbs and spices, that's fine; I don't because this ain't about trying to make something taste like it came from a damn French restaurant—we're talking about the basics of barbecue.) We bring that to a boil, we stir to dissolve the salt and sugar, and we let it cool. Then we submerge the whole chicken or turkey in the brine in a container large enough to hold it, and let it sit overnight in the refrigerator. (You can also put it in an ice-packed cooler.) When you're ready to cook it, take the bird out of the brine (discard the brine), then pat it dry thoroughly inside and out with paper towels or a clean dry kitchen towel. Rub that bird down inside and out with white vinegar. Then season it liberally with salt and pepper. Note that some birds, especially turkeys, have got a lot of thick skin, and you need the salt and pepper on there in a heavy coating.

SMOKED WHOLE CHICKEN

This is the best recipe for a beginner, the perfect place to get you started on your journey to becoming a pitmaster. The nicest part about it is that once you've got it mastered, you end up with something pretty damn impressive to serve your friends and family in the backyard—they don't need to know how easy it is to get this right. That said, there is one crucial thing you need to remember here:

Chickens like to dry out on the smoker, mostly because compared with pork shoulders, briskets, and ribs they just don't have a lot of fat on them. My chickens never dry out because I put a pan of apple juice underneath them in the smoker, which ensures that the chicken is bathed in moisture and sweetness for the duration of its cook time. (Note: This is not a recipe that's going to give you seared crunchy skin; the point of smoking a chicken is to produce meat so soft to bite through, you don't even need a knife to cut it.)

ingredients

1 (3½- to 4-pound) large whole chicken

4 cups Smoked Stock (page 93) or good-quality store-bought stock

2 cups Jack's Old South Huney Muney Cluck Rub or make your own (see page 73)

2 cups apple juice

Place the chicken in a deep baking pan, pour over the stock, and marinate, covered, in the refrigerator for at least three hours, or preferably overnight.

When are you ready to cook the chicken, preheat a smoker to 250°F.

Remove the pan from the refrigerator and pour out the stock. Pat the chicken dry all over with paper towels or a clean kitchen towel. Apply the rub liberally to the chicken, making sure to get it all over the bird. Place the chicken breast side up on a meat rack with the handles facing down, so the bird will be raised above the surface of the pans. Set the rack inside a deep aluminum pan. Pour the apple juice into the bottom of the pan, underneath the meat rack. Place the pan in the smoker and cook for 1½ hours. Pull the pan from the smoker. Using a sharp knife, cut off the wings of the bird (see page 88 for instructions on how to do that). Wrap the wings in aluminum foil and keep them warm in an oven on the lowest setting. Meanwhile, return the rest of the

recipe continues

chicken to the smoker and cook for an additional 1½ hours, or until the internal temperature of the white meat reaches 165°F and the dark meat reaches 180°F. Remove the chicken from the smoker and allow it to rest just as it is, on the rack in its pan and uncovered, for 15 minutes. To serve, carve the chicken into individual pieces.

Note: If you like to make pulled chicken to eat on its own or for pulled chicken sandwiches: Put on a pair of food-handling gloves. Over a cutting board, pull the chicken apart at the breastbone, applying firm pressure with your thumbs on either side of the bone while gently using the rest of your fingers to separate the breasts from the bone. Then pull the chicken meat from the bones and transfer to a platter. I like to make pulled chicken sandwiches by spreading both sides of a soft roll with barbecue sauce and then serving and eating those suckers immediately.

SMOKED HALF CHICKENS

SERVES 2

I have made it very clear that I ate lots of hog when I was growing up and very little of other meats—chicken and brisket both included. If I saw chicken that wasn't fried when I was a kid, it was made in the following fashion. That's because my dad loved to make half chickens, so I'm going to give you his method for that—that's what he sold for take-out in his barbecue business and what I saw him cooking when I was coming up.

ingredients

1 (3½- to 4-pound) whole chicken

1 recipe brine (page 104)

½ cup Jack's Old South Huney Muney Cluck Rub or make your own (see page 73)

¼ cup white vinegar

Kosher salt, to taste

Freshly ground black pepper, to taste

We buy whole chickens, local ones, and then we split them ourselves (see page 99). First, remove the neck and giblets. Place the chicken on a cutting board, breast side down. Using a very sharp kitchen knife, cleaver, or sharp kitchen shears and working from the cavity opening to the neck, cut down the backbone of each side of the chicken; discard the backbone. Next, cut a two-inch slit through the membrane and cartilage at the "V" of the neck end. Grab a breast in each hand and gently bend both sides backward, as if you were opening a book, to snap the breastbone. Use your fingers to work along both sides of the breastbone to loosen the triangular keel bone; pull out the bone. With the tip of a sharp knife, cut along both sides of the cartilage at the end of the breast-bone; remove the cartilage. Turn the chicken breast side up. The final step: Cut lengthwise down the center of the chicken to split it into two halves.

The chicken halves should be brined at least 4 hours, or preferably overnight (see page 104 for brine recipe), in gallon-size zip-top bags.

When ready to cook, remove the chicken halves from the brine. Pat the halves down with paper towels or a clean dry kitchen towel. Rub each chicken half inside and out, skin and cavity, with white vinegar. Then season them thoroughly all over with salt and pepper—take your time to season the chicken well.

recipe continues

Preheat a smoker to 250°F. Place the chicken, breast side up, in a deep aluminum pan. Place the pan in the smoker and cook for 90 minutes, or until the breast meat reaches 165°F on an instant-read thermometer. At the 90-minute mark, take a look at the chicken skin. Push down on the skin with your finger and see if the push leaves a dimple. If that happens, you're on the way to being done. The final check for doneness is to grab that chicken leg and gently twist it, and if it pulls away, then it is ready to go.

Remove the chicken halves from the smoker and allow to rest uncovered in the pan for 15 minutes. Then serve your birds— I give a half chicken per person.

Can I make good barbecue chicken in the oven?

Oven-baked barbecue chicken can also be very tasty. It will have neither that fire-kissed taste you get from grilling chicken (page 102) nor that smoke-kissed flavor I love so much (page 105), but it will become extra soft and sweet if you cook it right—and in this form it's a comfort-food classic. Do I crave baked barbecue chicken sometimes? Damn right I do, especially when it's cold outside.

OVEN-BAKED BARBECUE CHICKEN

SERVES 4

ingredients

2 cups Jack's Old South Tangy Sweet Sauce or make your own (see page 78)

¼ cup apricot preserves

1 clove garlic, crushed

1 dash hot sauce

1 (3½- to 4-pound) large chicken cut into eight pieces (2 breasts, 2 legs, 2 thighs, 2 wings)

½ cup apple cider vinegar

½ cup Jack's Old South Huney Muney Cluck Rub or make your own (see page 73)

Olive oil, for brushing

Preheat oven to 350°F.

In a medium saucepan, combine the sauce, preserves, garlic, and hot sauce and heat, stirring constantly, over medium heat for 5 to 10 minutes, or until thoroughly combined and very warm. Set aside.

Using a very sharp knife, cut the chicken breasts in half. Rub all of the pieces with apple cider vinegar, then apply the rub to the pieces, making sure to get it all over both sides and into the skin.

Brush olive oil on a large baking sheet. Place the chicken pieces skin side down on the pan. Roast for 25 minutes. Remove from the oven and brush the sauce all over the bottom of the pieces. Use a spatula to very gently flip the pieces over, taking care not to tear the chicken skin. Brush the skin of each piece with the sauce. Return the chicken to the oven for another 7 to 10 minutes to allow the sauce to set into the skin. Remove the pan from the oven once more. Increase the temperature in the oven to 425°F. While it is preheating, brush a final coating of sauce onto each piece, using up all the sauce.

Return the pan to the oven and continue roasting for another 5 to 10 minutes, or until the sauce browns around the edges and the chicken is cooked through. Remove the chicken from the oven and let rest, uncovered, for 10 minutes. Serve warm.

Why does the chicken on my chicken thighs always come out rubbery?

This is a very good question that comes up all the time when I'm giving cooking demonstrations and teaching classes. It's a legit issue: Sometimes the low cooking temperatures required for smoking are not hot enough to render the fat out of the skin of chicken thighs, and the skin becomes flabby and rubbery. You need a strategy, and here it is: Use a sharp knife to loosen a point of the skin of your chicken thigh, and then wedge a finger inside to loosen it all the way. Use your sharp knife and your finger to scrape the underside of the thigh skin, removing the excess fat in the process and taking care not to tear the skin. After you've scraped out the fat, reattach the skin and smoke those chicken thighs.

Can I make Buffalo chicken wings on a smoker?

I'm a wing man. If I had a nickel for every time I've said it, I'd be, well, a little bit richer. I eat 'em all the time, and I love 'em. I love most foods that have a handle, from pizza crusts to those little lamb chop lollipops. But chicken wings are special to me. Not only do they have *two* handles to hold onto—one on the flat and the other on the drumette—but they are delicious, and they're even better when they've got the flavor of smoke mixed in with the distinctive Buffalo sauce. Here's how to do it right:

SMOKED BUFFALO BARBECUE WINGS

ingredients

3 tablespoons Jack's Old South Tangy Sweet Sauce or make your own (see page 78)

3 tablespoons hot sauce

1 tablespoon plus 1 teaspoon unsalted butter, melted

12 chicken wings

Kosher salt, to taste

Freshly ground black pepper, to taste

Vegetable oil, for deep-frying

In a large bowl, combine the barbecue sauce, hot sauce, and melted butter. Set aside.

Using a very sharp knife, cut each wing in half to separate the flat from the drumette. Wash the pieces well in cold water, then pat them dry with paper towels or a clean kitchen towel. Season the wings on all sides with salt and pepper.

Heat a heavy, deep skillet, preferably cast-iron, over high heat. Pour enough oil into the hot skillet to come halfway up the sides. Heat the oil until it shimmers on its surface but is not smoking (if using an electric skillet, heat the oil to 350°F).

Using tongs, carefully place the wings in the hot oil, taking care not to tear their skins. Fry the wings, carefully turning them over halfway through, until their skins are golden brown, about 10 minutes.

Transfer the wings to paper towels to drain. Working in batches, quickly place them in the bowl of sauce and toss them thoroughly, until evenly coated. Get your favorite dipping sauce—I like ranch dressing myself—and a good cold beer and enjoy immediately.

HOW TO SEPARATE CHICKEN WINGS

Tip

Flat

Drumette

Q:

what is your favorite way to cook chicken breasts?

A:

Oh yes, the boneless, skinless chicken breast. People love to talk about how boring they are and how much thighs are better because they have more fat and flavor. But I'll be honest with you: Sometimes the comfort of a chicken cutlet is just what the doctor ordered, even for a pitmaster. However, I do find that unless you have a great plan for adding flavor to an otherwise pretty bland piece of meat, your boneless skinless chicken breast is likely to disappoint you. I have a solution for you: Bacon. I wrap my boneless, skinless chicken breast in bacon, and then I smoke it. And you cannot imagine a better chicken cutlet in this world than that.

SMOKED BACON-WRAPPED BONELESS, SKINLESS CHICKEN BREASTS

SERVES 2 TO 4

ingredients

4 medium-size boneless, skinless chicken breasts (about 2 pounds)

¼ cup apple cider vinegar

Kosher salt, to taste

Freshly ground black pepper, to taste

1 cup Smoked Stock (page 93) or good-quality store-bought stock

1 medium white onion, diced

2 gloves garlic, crushed

2 cups Jack's Old South Huney Muney Cluck Rub or make your own (see page 73)

8 thin slices smoked bacon

Rub the chicken breasts all over with apple cider vinegar. Season them on both sides with salt and pepper. Place the chicken breasts in a shallow dish or a gallon-size zip-top plastic bag. Add the stock, onion, and garlic. Cover or seal, and refrigerate at least 3 hours, or preferably overnight.

When you are ready to cook the chicken, heat the smoker to 325°F.

Remove the chicken from the marinade. Discard the marinade. Pat the chicken dry with paper towels or a clean kitchen towel. Apply the rub liberally, all over both sides of the chicken breasts. Wrap each breast in 2 slices of the bacon, securing the ends with toothpicks. Place the breasts in an aluminum baking pan. Place the pan in the smoker and cook the breasts for 1 hour, or until their internal temperature reaches 165°F.

Remove the pan from the smoker and let the breasts rest, uncovered, in the pan for 15 minutes. Then slice the breasts and garnish them with any bacon pieces that have fallen aside. Serve immediately. This is delicious with a cold beer.

Do you ever make stuffed chicken breasts on the smoker?

Someone asked me this recently on Facebook. In my experience people don't realize two things: just how many foods they can make in a smoker, and just how much smoking adds flavor to the foods and dishes they already know and love (see the Cornbread & Sausage Stuffing for another great example, page 130). Stuffed chicken breasts can be great when cooked in a smoker.

APPLE AND BACON-STUFFED CHICKEN BREASTS

SERVES 4

ingredients

1 green or yellow apple (preferably Golden Delicious), peeled, cored, and chopped

4 slices bacon, fried and crumbled

1 tablespoon fine dry breadcrumbs

⅓ cup Smoked Stock (page 93) or good-quality store-bought stock

Kosher salt, to taste

Freshly ground black pepper, to taste

4 large boneless, skinless chicken breasts (about 12 ounces each)

2 cups Jack's Old South Huney Muney Cluck Rub or make your own (see page 73)

1 cup apple juice

Preheat your smoker to 300°F.

In a small bowl, combine the apples, bacon, bread crumbs, and broth to form a loose stuffing. Season with salt and pepper. Set aside.

Season the breasts all over with salt and pepper. Using a sharp paring knife, cut a pocket about 3 inches deep in the thickest side of each chicken breast. Spoon the apple mixture in the pockets and secure the openings with toothpicks.

Apply the rub to the outside of the chicken breasts, taking care to get it all over on both sides. Transfer the breasts to a large aluminum pan, and place the pan in the smoker. Pour the apple juice into a spray bottle. Cook the chicken breasts for 1 hour, opening the smoker to spritz them all over with the apple juice every 15 minutes, or until the internal temperature of each breast reaches 165°F.

Remove the pan from the smoker and allow the chicken to rest, loosely tented with aluminum foil, for 10 minutes. Serve warm.

Can I smoke just the turkey drumsticks?

I love to go to a state fair or a big barbecue festival and eat one of those giant smoked turkey legs. It used to be unheard of to be able to go into a grocery store and buy pieces of a bird. When I was growing up—which ain't that long ago—you had to buy the whole damn bird and, if you liked drumsticks as much as I do, you had to hope your family and friends would go for the white meat so you could have them all to yourself. (That never happened in my house, because everyone thought the drumsticks were worth putting up a fight over.) Times are different now, of course. Especially because it's possible to buy turkey drumsticks—and I know a number of grocery stores and butchers who'll sell them to you directly—so you can smoke "just" those and make sure everyone who deserves one can have one.

SMOKED TURKEY DRUMSTICKS

ingredients

½ gallon water

½ cup kosher salt

¼ cup dark brown sugar

1 teaspoon ground allspice

1 teaspoon ground coriander

1 teaspoon dry mustard

4 large turkey drumsticks

2 tablespoons olive oil

2 tablespoons Jack's Old South Huney Muney Cluck Rub or make your own (see page 73)

1 cup Jack's Old South Tangy Sweet Sauce or make your own (see page 78)

Cure the legs overnight: In a large bowl, combine the water, salt, sugar, allspice, coriander, and mustard; stir to dissolve the seasonings. Pour the curing solution into a large zip-top plastic bag and add the turkey legs. Place the bag in a large aluminum baking pan and refrigerate for 24 hours.

When ready to cook the turkey legs, preheat a smoker to 250°F.

Remove the turkey legs from the curing liquid and rinse off in cold water. Discard the curing liquid. Pat the legs dry with paper towels. Coat the legs with the olive oil, then, using your fingers, lightly coat them with the rub.

Place the legs back into the aluminum baking pan, cover the pan with foil, and place the plan in the smoker, close the smoker, and cook the legs for 3 hours, or until the temperature of the legs reads 180°F on an instant-read thermometer. To crisp the skin of the legs, uncover the pan and leave the drumsticks on the smoker for 15 additional minutes after the internal temperature has reached 180°F. (Alternately, you can transfer the legs to an oven that's been preheated to 400°F and cook them, watching carefully to make sure the skin does not burn, for about 10 additional minutes.)

Pull the pan out of the smoker. Wrap each leg in foil and let rest for 10 minutes. Remove the foil and serve, with barbecue sauce on the side for dipping, if you like.

Even though you're a barbecue pitmaster,
do you ever make fried chicken?

Listen, fried chicken is probably my favorite food on the planet. Yes, I know the planet also contains barbecue. But man cannot live on barbecue alone. Fried chicken is the official dish of the South, I grew up on it, and I cannot get enough of it—and that's the truth about me. So you bet that I know how to make it, and my version is damn near perfect, too. One of the not-so-secret things about fried chicken that any real Southerner can tell you is that you have to soak the chicken overnight in buttermilk for that special sweet-sour flavor to soak into the meat and keep it moist. My second not-so-secret tip for perfect fried chicken is to fry it in lard. I'm talking real rendered pork fat, the kind you need to have real hogs around you to produce. (Or at least have a good butcher who can get you some—whatever you do, don't buy packaged boxes of lard from the grocery store; get the real thing from a butcher.) Finally, I like to fry birds that are small and young because I think they have a much better flavor than older, larger birds do—you can save those suckers for stewing or whatever the hell those fancy chefs do.

SOUTHERN FRIED CHICKEN

SERVES 4

If you absolutely cannot find fresh pork lard from a butcher in your area, you can substitute peanut oil in its place.

ingredients

1 (3-pound) small chicken, cut into 8 pieces (2 legs, 2 thighs, 2 wings, 2 breasts)

4 cups buttermilk

2 cups all-purpose flour

1 tablespoon kosher salt

2 tablespoons freshly ground black pepper

1 teaspoon garlic powder

1 teaspoon onion powder

1 teaspoon chili powder

1 teaspoon sugar

1 teaspoon paprika

2 large eggs

1 to 1½ cups pork lard

Divide the chicken pieces into two gallon-size zip-top plastic bags. Pour 2 cups of buttermilk into each bag. Seal the bags well and refrigerate for at least 3 hours, or preferably overnight.

When you're ready to cook the chicken: In a large bowl, combine the flour, salt, pepper, garlic, onion, and chili powder, sugar, and paprika. Use your fingers or a fork to combine all of the ingredients. Set aside. In another large bowl, beat the eggs.

Transfer chicken pieces from the buttermilk mixture to a platter, taking care to pat them dry with paper towels or a clean kitchen towel. Dredge the chicken pieces in the egg, and then coat them in the seasoned flour. Repeat the process with each piece, dredging it first in the egg and then coating in the seasoned flour, so that each piece has been dipped and coated twice and has a double layer of batter on it. Set the pieces on the platter.

Heat a large deep cast-iron skillet over medium heat. Melt the lard in the pan, making sure it's at least 1 inch deep. Allow the lard to reach 350°F on a deep-fry thermometer and be completely melted. The pan should be hot but not smoking—don't let the oil smoke. When the pan is hot enough, add the chicken pieces to the skillet in batches, cooking each batch for about 18 minutes, turning the pieces halfway through the cooking time (except the wings, which will need only about 5 minutes on each side). Drain the chicken pieces thoroughly on paper towels. Serve warm or at room temperature, depending on your taste.

Q:

Can I make my Thanksgiving turkey on the smoker?

A:

You're damn right you can. And there are a lot of advantages to smoking your turkey. The biggest one is that if you cook the bird outdoors on the smoker, you leave room for all your Thanksgiving sides in the oven—and that's important. The other reason is that because turkey meat tastes pretty bland, smoking the bird really improves its flavor. The one thing you have to worry about is drying out the bird. But do not worry. If you follow my instructions, your bird will turn out just perfectly—smoking it with the pan of apple juice underneath it takes care of that problem. Also, even if you follow my Thanksgiving plan, I'd like to encourage you not to wait until Thanksgiving to smoke a turkey. It's delicious any time of year.

SMOKED THANKSGIVING

PITMASTER-STYLE DEVILED EGGS *(page 293)*

SMOKED TURKEY *(page 126)*

CORNBREAD & SAUSAGE STUFFING *(page 130)*

SMOKED SWEET POTATOES *(page 131)*

BARBECUED CABBAGE *(page 132)*

SMOKED TURKEY

SERVES 10 TO 12

This is the main event right here, the big bird you want to serve for the big day. I'm going to tell you how to do it up so that you'll never want to cook it in the oven again.

ingredients

1 (12- to 15-pound) turkey, neck and giblets removed

8 cups Smoked Stock (page 93) or good-quality store-bought stock

3 medium white onions, diced

4 cloves garlic, crushed

1 cup packed dark brown sugar

1 cup kosher salt

2 cups Jack's Old South Huney Muney Cluck Rub or make your own (see page 73)

2 cups apple juice

Make a brine for the turkey: In a large stockpot combine the chicken stock, onions, garlic, and brown sugar. Bring to a boil over high heat. Remove the pot from the heat and let the brine cool completely. Place the turkey in a large roasting bag or a clean cooler or other large container, and carefully pour the brine into the container or bag. Seal the container or the tie the bag. Refrigerate, allowing the turkey to sit in the brine at least 8 hours, or preferably overnight.

When you are ready to cook the turkey, preheat a smoker to 250°F.

Remove the turkey from the brine. Discard the brine. Pat the bird dry thoroughly with paper towels or a clean kitchen towel. Apply the rub all over the bird, inside and out.

Set a roasting rack inside a deep aluminum pan with the handles facing down, so the bird will be raised. Pour the apple juice into the bottom of the pan, underneath the meat rack. Place the turkey on the rack. Place the pan in the smoker and cook for 5 hours, or until the breast meat of the turkey reaches an internal temperature of 165°F.

Remove the pan from the smoker. Allow the turkey to rest, loosely covered with foil, for 30 minutes. Carve the turkey and serve immediately.

HOW TO CARVE A TURKEY

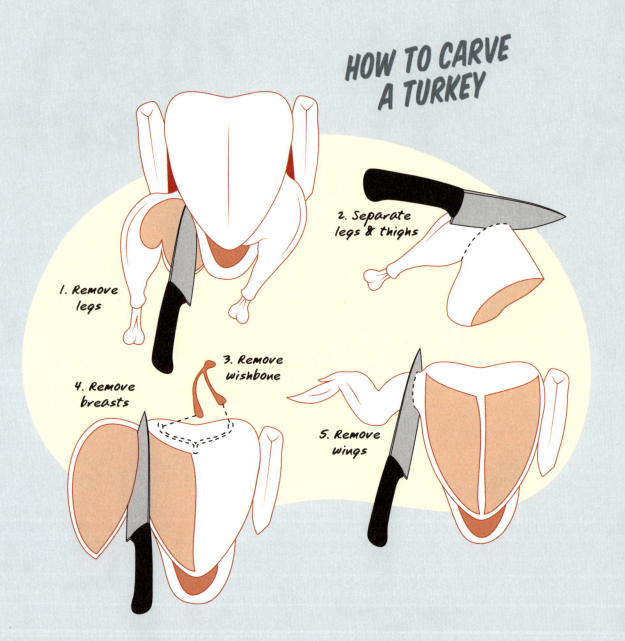

1. Remove legs

2. Separate legs & thighs

3. Remove wishbone

4. Remove breasts

5. Remove wings

A NOTE ON CARVING

There is a better way to carve a turkey that will not leave the uncarved portion sitting out on your counter drying out while you eat. **Do not try to carve your turkey by slicing vertically or diagonally along the breast the way you've seen people do it your whole life.** Do it this way instead:

Step One: Cut off the turkey breast—that's right, remove the whole breast from the bird.

Step Two: Cut slices across the breast horizontally, using short strokes instead of long strokes, so you're cutting across the grain. Your turkey meat will be so much more moist, tender, and juicy this way. You can thank me later.

1. Remove entire breast

2. Slice breast against the grain

HOW TO REMOVE A TURKEY BREAST

CORNBREAD & SAUSAGE STUFFING

SERVES 10 TO 12

I know you've all heard of "stovetop stuffing"—but this here is smoker stuffing. The advantage to cooking your stuffing in the smoker is that it will acquire the smoky-sweet flavors of the turkey and the apple juice as it cooks, which will make it pair so well with your smoked bird. Try it, and thank me later. This recipe is for a classic sausage stuffing. I like to make mine with cornbread, but you can use sourdough or any other style of bread that you like instead.

ingredients

2½ pounds cornbread or other favorite bread, cut into ¾-inch dice (about 5 quarts)

8 tablespoons butter (1 stick)

1½ pounds pork sausage, preferably flavored with sage, removed from casing

1 large white onion, finely chopped

4 large stalks celery, finely chopped

4 cloves garlic, minced

2 teaspoons dried sage

Kosher salt, to taste

Freshly ground black pepper, to taste

1 quart Smoked Stock (page 93) or good-quality store-bought stock

If you're making this as part of the whole menu, your smoker should be set at 250°F with your Thanksgiving turkey in it. If not, preheat a smoker to 250°F. Spread the bread cubes evenly over 2 baking sheets. Bake until the bread is completely toasted and dried, 50 minutes, rotating the pans halfway through the cooking time. Remove the bread cubes from the oven and allow them to cool completely.

In a large Dutch oven, melt the butter over medium-high heat until foaming subsides (do not allow butter to brown), about 2 minutes. Add the sausage and mash with a stiff whisk or potato masher to break it up into fine pieces (the largest pieces should be no bigger than ¼ inch). Cook, stirring frequently, until only a few bits of pink remain, about 8 minutes. Add the onion, celery, garlic, sage, and salt and pepper and cook, stirring frequently, until the vegetables are softened, about 10 minutes. Remove from the heat and stir in the chicken stock. Add the bread cubes and fold gently until evenly mixed.

Spoon the stuffing into a 13 by 9-inch aluminum baking pan. Cover the pan with foil and place in your prepared smoker. Smoke the stuffing for 1½ hours, or until heated through. Serve with your Thanksgiving turkey.

SMOKED SWEET POTATOES

SERVES 10 TO 12

ingredients

12 large sweet potatoes

8 tablespoons (1 stick) unsalted butter, melted

3 tablespoons Jack's Old South Huney Muney Cluck Rub or make your own (see page 73)

Your favorite toppings, such as marshmallows, ground cinnamon, and ground nutmeg, or butter, sour cream, and salt and pepper

If you're making this as part of the whole menu, your smoker should be set at 250°F with your Thanksgiving turkey in it. If not, preheat a smoker to 250°F.

Wash the sweet potatoes thoroughly, scrubbing any dirt from their skins, and dry them with paper towels or a clean kitchen towel. Prick each sweet potato with a fork so that steam can escape during baking. Brush the sweet potatoes all over with the melted butter and season them all over with the rub.

Place the sweet potatoes in a large deep aluminum baking pan and cover with aluminum foil. Smoke the potatoes until they are cooked through, about 2 hours; the skins will be crisp and the potatoes will yield to the touch and feel soft in the center.

Wrap the potatoes individually in aluminum foil to keep them warm until ready to serve. Serve with your favorite toppings.

BARBECUED CABBAGE

SERVES 10 TO 12

This delicious side dish is like a pitmaster's version of sauerkraut, and it adds some welcome acidity to your rich Thanksgiving dinner. It's also as simple as can be to prepare a couple of heads of cabbage the day before Thanksgiving and then just toss them onto the smoker right alongside your turkey and stuffing.

ingredients

2 very large or 3 small-to-medium heads of green cabbage

2 tablespoons kosher salt

2 teaspoons freshly ground black pepper

2 teaspoons garlic powder

2 teaspoons Jack's Old South Original Rub or make your own (see page 72)

1 cup (2 sticks) unsalted butter

If you're making this as part of the whole menu, your smoker should be set at 250°F with your Thanksgiving turkey in it. If not, preheat a smoker to 250°F.

Use a very sharp knife to core the cabbages and remove their tough white bottoms. You should be left with whole round cabbages that have only their center cores removed—they will still be in the shape of globes. Carefully rinse the cored cabbages in cold water and pull off any wilted exterior leaves. Pat the cabbages dry with paper towels or a clean kitchen towel. Sprinkle the salt, pepper, garlic powder, and rub into the hollowed centers of the cabbages. Place a stick of butter inside the center of each cabbage where the core was removed and on top of the spices you just sprinkled.

Wrap each head of cabbage in aluminum foil with the core end up. Using more foil, form a solid base to help the cabbages stand upright. Place the wrapped cabbages in the smoker. Cover and smoke for 4 to 6 hours, or until the cabbages are soft. Unwrap the cabbages and discard any blackened leaves. Cut the cabbages into quarters and serve them alongside the smoked turkey.

HOW TO BARBECUE A CABBAGE

1. Core the cabbage

2. Add seasonings and butter

3. Wrap in foil

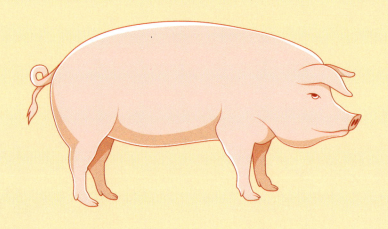

THE WHOLE HOG

ALL ABOUT COOKING THE PIG

Tenderloin

Loin

Belly

Ham

St. Louis Ribs

Baby Back Ribs

Jowl

Shoulder & Boston Butt

PART ONE

SMOKING A WHOLE HOG

Why should I smoke a whole hog?

This is not a stupid question: Smoking a whole hog is no joke. If you're going to do it, you need to make a forty-eight-hour commitment to the process. And I'm not going to tell you it's easy. (What I will share are all the ways to make smoking a whole hog easier for you, and if you're already sold on doing it, turn to page 144 and follow my instructions.)

Why should you do it? For the same reason people compete in an Ironman Triathlon, or NASCAR drivers want to win the Indianapolis 500, or runners want to complete the New York City marathon. Smoking a whole hog is about as legit as any barbecuer can get, and that counts for folks who are backyard enthusiasts all the way on up to professional pitmasters like me.

So why smoke a whole hog?

— Because you want to show up, show out, and impress your family, friends, and neighbors by feeding a hundred or so of them in high style

— Because you want to up your barbecue game and increase your smoking skills

— Because you like doing badass things, and smoking a whole hog is as badass as cooking gets

My advice: Stop thinking about finally getting around to smoking a whole hog with that new smoker you just bought, or with the one that's sitting there rusting in your backyard, and get to it. You will thank me later, I promise you.

How do I go about getting a whole hog?

You've noticed no doubt that you can't just march into your local Piggly Wiggly and buy a whole hog. You can't even do that anymore in South Georgia, where I live, where there used to be more roadside barbecue stands, just like the one my daddy owned and operated, than I could count. Back then you knew a local hog farmer, and you struck up a deal for yourself. But here we are, and you want to buy a whole hog. Here's what you need to know:

A whole hog can weigh between 75 and 180 or so pounds, give or take. I prefer ones on the big side, because if I'm going to smoke a whole hog I'm usually trying to feed a big crowd. I don't pay any mind to the folks who say smaller is better because smaller hogs are easier to handle—it's not a particularly different experience, so I figure that if you're going to smoke a whole hog, you should get as much out of it as you can for all the work you're going to put into it.

STEP ONE: FIND YOURSELF A GOOD LOCAL FARMER AND A GOOD BUTCHER.

Relationships with farmers and butchers are important to people who cook professionally, and you might want to consider making them important to you as well. As for me, I buy my hogs from a local Mennonite butcher named Elmer Yoder; his business is not far from my home and is called Yoder's Butcher Block. I call him up on the phone regularly to ask questions and get good advice on hogs. You can try calling him, too, and if you're awfully nice to him, you might try to convince him to ship one to you—although, frankly, you both would find it easier if you bought one locally. When you find a good local butcher who can get you a whole hog, you can be much more sure that you're getting meat that's been as naturally raised as possible—I cook hormone-free, drug-free hogs only, and I advise you to do the same.

In all fifty states, livestock producers who want to sell must have the livestock slaughtered and processed at a USDA-inspected facility. In some states, though, it is permissible for livestock producers to sell what's known as "live" animals, which customers can have processed at a "custom-exempt" state-licensed facility. (Note: This is how meat shares and meat CSAs are possible in many states.) So technically you become the owner of a live animal before it's slaughtered, and then you either hire someone to butcher the animal for you, or you do it yourself. Different areas of the country have higher and lower percentages of farmers who will sell whole animals directly to consumers, and some don't allow farmers to do so at all. First, you need to find out if it's possible. Contact your state department of agriculture to find out if custom-exempt livestock sale and processing are allowed. You can find every state department of agriculture's contact information listed on the USDA's website (usda.gov).

A much easier option, in my opinion, is asking around at your local farmers' market. If live animal purchasing is allowed in your state, farmers there are probably selling meat this way. You can search online for farmers who will sell directly to you on localharvest.org, an online directory that matches consumers to more than thirty thousand farmers' markets and local farmers in their area.

Once you find someone who'll sell you a whole hog, there are a few questions you probably want to ask:

How are the pigs raised: in pastures or pens? Pastures are far better, for obvious reasons.

What are they fed: Wheat? Barley? Corn? Peas? Kitchen scraps? The more varied and natural the diet, the greater the chances are that you'll get a pig with a good meat-to-fat ratio and thus, the better your meat is going to taste.

How old are the pigs when they're slaughtered? I prefer older, bigger pigs because they have more fat on them, and fat is what makes your meat taste delicious.

Most important: Are the animals slaughtered on the farm, or can the farmer help arrange slaughtering for you? I prefer the animals to be slaughtered on the farm.

A note about cost: You should expect to pay somewhere in the range of $2.50 to $5.50 per pound for a whole hog. Remember that the weight of the hog includes its bones, cartilage, and skin, not just the meat. Start thinking about how you're going to use that stuff, too.

STEP TWO: DETERMINE THE HOG SIZE YOU NEED.

This is easier than you think because the size of the hog you can smoke depends entirely on the size that will fit into your smoker. To figure that out, measure the length inside your cooking chamber—make sure you measure inside, not outside. The inside of your smoking chamber needs to be at least four feet long to be able to accommodate the smallest hog, which will be somewhere between fifty and eighty pounds. If you want to cook a bigger one, you need five to six feet.

STEP THREE: COMMUNICATE WITH YOUR BUTCHER ABOUT THE CUT.

If you're going the direct-from-farmer route, you're in luck: Most slaughterhouses will handle the butchery for you. (And they'll charge you for it, too, so factor that in—it's usually thirty cents on up to a dollar per pound.) When you're ordering a whole hog, be sure to communicate that you want the hog to be "round," which means split and gutted. This will save you the hassle and trouble of dealing with animal viscera. Mainly for presentation purposes, I like to request the head to be left on and for the feet to be removed—but that part is up to you. And note that if you have the feet removed, make sure to still get them—not only did you pay for them, but trotters (and you'll get four of them) are a delicacy, and they contain a lot of gelatin that makes for very good stock.

Now that you've got a whole hog, you're ready to cook it. So let's go.

Why do you inject a whole hog?

Over the many years I've been cooking competitive barbecue, I have developed a hog-smoking method I can depend on: It's won me fame and fortune, so you should count on it, too. People don't believe me when I tell them that my hogs come out the same way every time I smoke them, but it's true. Part of that is because I cook them the same way every time. *I cook a whole hog on its back and I never turn it over.* This way, I can keep the hog's flavors contained, because the animal's thick skin acts as a kind of bowl. Injecting hogs with a brine-like solution is part of the plan here: The skin of the hog, in addition to its unchanging position on the smoker, holds in the juices and flavors I inject into the meat—that's why my pork is never dried out and is always tender and delicious.

You'll see a lot of people cook a whole hog with the pig's back up and belly down on the smoker, and even some cooks who flip the whole hog halfway through the smoking process. But my method of smoking hogs on their backs is what's worked for me and won me money consistently year and after year, and I can guarantee that if you do it this way, you won't have dried-out meat.

Note: Make sure you review my information about why I use a water pan in my smoker before you get started with your whole hog (page 51); for me, this is essential to my type of cooking a hog and you should understand why before you start this project.

SMOKED WHOLE HOG

SERVES 125 PEOPLE

ingredients

1 (180-pound) hog, gutted and split

3 x recipe Pork Marinade for injection (page 68)

9 cups Jack's Old South Original Rub or make your own (see page 72)

3 x recipe Pork Glaze (page 75)

tools

1 sharpened butcher knife

1 sharpened paring knife

Myron Mixon Rib Skimmer (optional)

1 meat saw

1 heavy-duty meat injector

1 kitchen brush, for basting (not a delicate flimsy one—more like a large, fresh paint brush)

2 (5- to 6-pound) inexpensive boneless pork shoulders (Boston butt only) or 2 brisket flats, which will support the hog in the smoker (you will not eat these)

1 to 3 helper humans, needed for carrying the whole hog

Prep the hog: On a long table covered with clean butcher paper or other sanitary covering, lay long strips of aluminum foil until the table is completely covered. Place the hog, which has been butchered and split with its head on and its feet removed, flat on its back on top of the foil.

Score the hog: With a sharp chef's knife, make shallow cuts in a crisscross pattern in the meat all along each side of the spine of the hog, especially making sure to create squares where the ribs connect to the spine. Then crack and pull down each side of the hog, starting from the spine. You want the hog to be laying semi-flat (or as flat as you can get it, without removing the sides from the spine), so that you can easily reach inside it.

Remove the membrane (or "silver") from the backs of the ribs on each side: The easiest way to do that is to make a small incision just below the length of the breastbone. Work your fingers underneath the membrane until you have 2 to 3 inches cleared. Grab the membrane with one of my rib skimmers or a towel or your fingers and gently but firmly pull it away from the ribs. Pulling off the membrane exposes loose fat that will need trimming, so take your sharp paring knife and cut away any excess exposed fat.

Use a meat saw to split and saw down in between the ribs and down each side of the spine of the hog. You're going to cut the ribs on both sides 3 inches off the spine. Why? Doing this makes baby back ribs out of full-size spareribs. Take care to saw only the bone, and try not to pierce the skin on the bottom of the hog. This will ultimately make it easier for you to serve the ribs.

recipe continues

SCORE & CRACK THE HOG

Score on both sides of spine

Ribs are cracked but still attached to spine

REMOVING RIB SILVER

SAWING THE BABY BACKS

Make cut 3 inches from the spine

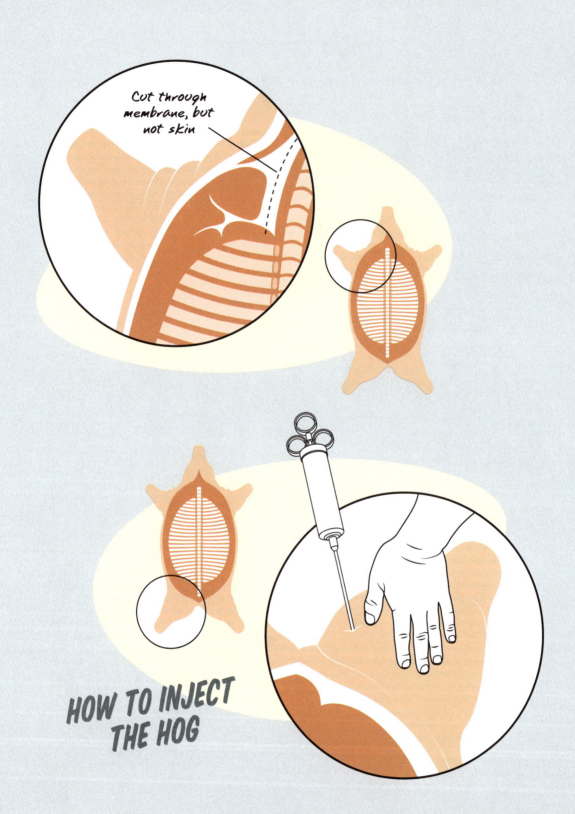

HOW TO INJECT
THE HOG

Separate the picnic ham of the shoulder from the Boston butt: First, use your sharp paring knife to trim both hams of any excess fat. Next, find the thick white membrane that separates the Boston butt end of the ham from the picnic end, which is next to the spine. Use your sharp butcher knife to cut right through the membrane, making sure not to cut through the hog skin. You're doing this so the shoulder can lay more flatly in the smoker and then crust over and form a good bark.

Inject the hog: Funnel the prepared Pork Marinade into your injector. I always start by injecting the hams first—making seven injections as evenly spaced as I can get them into each ham. Next, work your way up to the pig's head, making injections all along the side of the hog: It doesn't matter exactly where you make the injections as long as you evenly space them all over the animal.

Note: Don't make more injection holes than you need to get through your batch of injection liquid. More holes can mean more places for the injection to leak out. To do it right, move to the side of the cavity where the bacon is, the area that is covered by the hog's ribs. Inject all along both sides of that. Next, find the two tenderloins at the end of the spine, near the hams. Inject each one carefully and do not overinject the tenderloins—if the fluid begins leaking out, you'll know that you've done more than enough. Next, move to the shortened ribs that have been cut: Inject straight down between the ribs and directly against the spine, into the loin. Remember not to push the needle

through the skin on the bottom of the hog's back. Now, inject the shoulder, butt, and picnic ham. Last, inject the cheek meat (jowl) along the hog's jawbone.

Rub the hog: Sprinkle the rub throughout the hog's cavity and on the surface of any exposed meat. Gather up the foil you've laid the hog down on and use it to loosely wrap the whole hog all over. Let the hog sit for 1 hour to "marinate" in its injections. During this time, light your smoker and bring it to 250°F. (Instructions for how to do that are on pages 57 and 58.)

Place the two inexpensive pork shoulders or briskets you've reserved in the smoker, then carefully center the hog on top of them. You want that extra meat to be directly under the center of the hog. Close the smoker and let the hog smoke for about 20 hours, or until the internal temperature of the meatiest part of the shoulder registers 205°F on a meat thermometer.

Note: I often set my hog on the smoker at noon the day before I want to eat it, then I remove it at eight o'clock the following morning. If you do it that way, you can serve it for a big lunch for your family, friends, church crowd, political rally, whatever.

Unwrap the foil and use your new paintbrush to apply the pork glaze throughout the inside of the cavity and on the hams. Rewrap the hog loosely in the foil. Leaving the hog on the

recipe continues

smoker, let the temperature fall naturally—you don't need to feed your smoker any more wood at this point. The glaze will caramelize and set while the hog rests. I like to leave the hog on my smoker for my guests to come to and pick and pull meat right from there: That way you don't have to worry about moving a whole hog any more than you absolutely need to.

After about four hours of resting, your hog is ready to eat. In South Georgia, where I live, we don't "carve" a whole hog. We have a pig pickin', and pitmasters like me put on heavy gloves and use either tongs or our hands to gently pull the meat out of the hog in chunks and pile it onto platters and plates.

Note: The meat will be fairly warm, and you do need to be aware that there will be juices and grease from the hog to contend with—you can solve those problems the way some pitmasters do: Spread some sawdust or mulch on the ground underneath the table that's holding the whole hog to catch the grease that spills when folks are pulling the meat.

WHAT ARE TIPS FOR COOKING THE LOIN PROPERLY ON A WHOLE HOG?

If I had to name the single biggest pitfall of smoking a whole hog, it might just be overcooking the loin. The loin is pretty lean and doesn't have a lot of fat on it, and it's also the hog's most tender cut. And so paying special attention to keeping it tender after twenty or so hours of smoking is important. That's why you inject the loin—just make sure you don't do it too much. To make sure you're not injecting too much fluid, notice exactly when the fluid begins leaking out of the injection site and then stop—you will have done more than enough. You're going to keep your smoker heat at 250°F and make sure it doesn't burn any hotter. Finally, you are NOT going to skip the step where I tell you to buy those extra pork shoulders or briskets to prop up the underside of the hog. Doing this positions the hog so that the loins are protected inside the hog and won't dry out during the smoking process. Think about it: I cook my hogs on their backs, then I'll take a boneless pork butt and put it under its back, which covers the loins. This will prevent the loins from getting overcooked.

This is how we turn in ribs at a competition. See page 189 for the recipe.

Q:

Can I make homemade crackling pork skins?

A:

I've heard about a lot of first-time whole hog cooks who make one big mistake: They throw away the pigskin. Do not do that, for you will be robbing yourself of one of the most delicious snacks on planet Earth. Cracklin' pigskins are God's gift to pitmasters. Here's how I make mine:

CRACKLIN' PIGSKINS

This recipe can easily be doubled or tripled, depending on how much pigskin you are able to get your hands on.

ingredients

About 1½ pounds hog skin from a whole hog or shoulder or belly

⅓ cup kosher salt

Preheat the oven to 300°F.

Using a sharp paring knife, scrape any fat off the skin. Using kitchen shears, cut the skin into 1-inch pieces, about the size and shape of Triscuits, or as close to that ideal as you can make them. Place the skin pieces on top of a wire rack set in a large sheet pan and sprinkle them all over with the salt. Cook the skins in the oven until all of the fat is rendered in the bottom of the sheet pan and the skins have become golden brown and crispy—this usually takes about 3½ hours.

When the skins are golden and crispy, remove the pan from the oven. Transfer the skins to paper towels to further drain and to cool.

Dust the cracklin' skins with your favorite barbecue rub (or make your own, page 72) and dip them in your favorite barbecue sauce (or make your own, page 77), if you like.

PART TWO

PORK BEYOND THE HOG

Pork shoulders on a masonry pit.
Ain't they beautiful?

Q:

what kind of pork should I buy?

A:

There are two things to consider here: the quality of your pork, which I cover on page 140, and the cut you want to smoke, which I'll cover here. Before you spend your money with even the highest-quality producer or distributor of pork, I strongly suggest that you learn about the top cuts for smoking: The more you know about, say, where the chops come from or where the shoulder comes from, the more likely you are to master how to cook each one. Here's a great diagram:

Fatback
Salt pork
Pork chops
BB ribs
Butt
Rump
Loin
Shoulder blade
Leg
Ear
Tenderloin
Shank end
Spare rib
Arm
Ham
Head
Belly
Bacon side
Picnic ham
Hock
Hock
Jowl
HOG CUTS

While sourcing a whole hog is a special process (see page 140), individual cuts are a lot easier—although some of the same advice still applies in terms of finding a good local producer and a good local butcher. What I'm going to tell you here is true for buying just about every cut of pork there is, from the shoulder (which is the most traditional for pulled pork) to the chops, to the tenderloin, to both kinds of ribs: It goes without saying that to make championship barbecue, you *must* start with quality product. The single best piece of advice I can give you: Get to know your local butcher. He or she has access to the freshest meat, and as you build a working relationship, he or she can steer you to the best cuts and the best meats.

For Pork Shoulder: A "pork shoulder" is the term for the top of the front leg of the hog—which isn't exactly the hog's "shoulder," but it's close enough. Each side of a pig has a *Boston butt* (the upper part, also called the Boston blade roast) and a *picnic* (the lower part of the leg), both of which can be transformed into roasts, stews, or ground meat. Grocery-store butchers and other mass meat marketers usually split both the Boston butt and the picnic into two or three smaller roasts (some will be on the bone, some boneless), or they'll turn the picnic into stew meat or ground pork. Of the picnic and the Boston butt, the Boston butt is marbled throughout and full of good fat, and it's the more ideal of the two for smoking. However, for smoking professionally at contests, or just in your backyard to feed the largest number of people, use a whole shoulder. I'm going to tell you how to smoke all three, but know that a good butcher should be able to get a whole shoulder, a Boston butt, or a picnic ham for you with no problem. If he or she can't, you've got the wrong butcher and you need to find a better one.

For Pork Chops: All pork chops come from the loin of the pig, which is the section that runs from the hip to the shoulder and also contains the small strip of meat called the *tenderloin*. If you were looking at a pig horizontally, the loin is the part that's right beneath the back (and that good back fat that protects and flavors the meat). The center cut, or pork loin chop, has a large T-shaped bone in the center of it—just like a T-bone steak does. Pork rib chops come, as their name suggests, from the rib portion of the loin. Each side of the pig has between fifteen and thirty chops, depending on how the butchering is done (for example, how thick the chops are cut and whether they're boneless or bone-in). Baby back ribs are the set of ribs from the loin that are cut away from the spine (see page 179 for more on ribs).

For Pork Belly: When a pig is slaughtered, it is always split down the middle in order to safely remove the innards—that's the proper protocol. That means there are always two bellies, one on each side, of a hog. When a belly is cured, smoked, and sliced, it becomes your bacon. **Spareribs** lie underneath the front portion of the belly cut. Those are your St. Louis ribs, and you can learn to cook them on page 189.

OTHER CUTS:

Pork Jowl is a triangular cut from underneath the pig's head, from the area between its lips and its shoulder. If a hog had a chin or a neck to speak of, this would be it. The cheek meat is sometimes included in the jowl, and the cheek is an extremely tender and choice part of the hog. I like to add some jowl meat when I cook my collard greens (see page 303 for the recipe), but you can find salt-cured smoked jowl bacon (called guanciale in Italian) on the menu at Italian delis as well as in fine Italian restaurants and high-end butcher shops. It's delicious.

Pork Trotters are, of course, the pig's feet. You get four of them per pig if you buy a whole hog (see page 140 if you're interested in doing that), but you can special-order trotters from a good butcher. Personally, I love smoking trotters and eating them, too. It's a very old-school barbecue pitmaster thing to do, right there. I usually do that only when I'm barbecuing in my masonry pits. I wrote a book about how to build a pit in your backyard like the kind my dad used to cook with, which you can do with very little aggravation and for less than $300—but you've got to buy that book to find out how: It's called *Myron Mixon's BBQ Rules: The Old-School Guide to Smoking Meat.*

How do I smoke a pork shoulder?

The first big-money contests I learned to cook for were all sanctioned by the Memphis Barbecue Network organization. (The other big barbecue contest sanctioning body is the Kansas City Barbecue Society, and I've won more of their contests than I can count, too.) At MBN contests, you can either use a whole shoulder or the Boston butt by itself. I'm used to cooking the whole thing, so that's what I've always done. And I recommend it to you because it's no small thing to smoke a pig shoulder, so if you're going to go ahead and do it, you should get as much out of it and feed as many folks (or provide as many meals for yourself) as you can. You may need to order a whole shoulder from a butcher—it can be hard to find in supermarkets outside the Barbecue Belt. Check my guidelines on ordering whole hogs if you want to get the freshest, most locally sourced shoulder you can (page 140).

SMOKED WHOLE PORK SHOULDER

ingredients

1 (18- to 20-pound) pork shoulder, including the Boston butt and picnic ham in one cut

3 x recipe Pork Marinade for injection (page 68)

3 cups Jack's Old South Original Rub or make your own (see page 72)

1 cup apple juice

1 recipe Pork Glaze (page 75)

tools

1 solid cutting board

1 sharp boning or pairing knife

2 aluminum baking pans

1 heavy-duty meat injector

Lay your pork shoulder on a clean workspace. Use a sharp paring knife to trim away any bone slivers from the exposed meat, and any excess fat. Your goal is to "square up" the long sides of the shoulder to make it as uniform and as easy to handle as you can get it.

Place the shoulder in a large deep aluminum pan. Prepare your pork marinade and load it into your injector. Inject the shoulder with 2 to 3 quarts of the injection, using the larger amount for bigger shoulders. You want to make your injections all over the shoulder, about 1 square inch away from one another. Let the injected shoulder "marinate" while injected, loosely covered, in the refrigerator for 2 hours.

After 2 hours, remove the shoulder from the refrigerator. Turn it upside down in the pan so that any excess injection can infuse the meat. Let it sit upside down for 15 to 20 minutes. Meanwhile, prepare your smoker and heat it to 250°F.

Take the shoulder out of the pan and sprinkle the rub all over it, making sure to get the area by the shank (you can see two round shank bones that are exposed on both ends; it will be the wider, less narrow end). Place the shoulder in its pan again, and put it in the smoker. Smoke it uncovered for 3 hours without opening the smoker if possible.

After 3 hours, remove the shoulder from the smoker. Pour the apple juice into a clean aluminum pan and transfer the shoulder into the new pan. Discard the old pan. Cover the shoulder in its new pan with foil and place it in the smoker. Cook for 6 hours, or until the internal temperature of the thickest part of the shoulder reads 205°F.

recipe continues

Remove the pan from the smoker. Discard the foil covering. Brush the pork glaze all over both sides of the shoulder. Return the shoulder to the pan, put the pan back in the smoker and smoke uncovered for 1 hour while adding no more heat to the smoker and allowing the internal temperature of the smoker to drop. The shoulder will effectively be resting in the smoker this way.

After 1 hour, remove the pan from the smoker and serve your shoulder in your favorite way.

Here in South Georgia, we don't slice our shoulders—we pull them apart in chunks (hence the name "pulled pork"). But if you like slices, feel free. Otherwise, you can use butcher knives or tongs or put some heavy gloves on your hands and pull that meat apart. You can pile it on platters and let guests make pulled pork sandwiches, or you can further chop up the meat (for "chopped pulled pork") after you've pulled it, if you like.

CAN I MAKE A PORK SHOULDER IN THE OVEN?

Yes, you can. Follow the instructions on page 162 for Simple Smoked Pork Shoulder. Marinate the meat as directed. Instead of preparing a smoker, preheat the oven to 300°F. When the oven is ready, discard the marinade, then pat the meat dry with paper towels or a clean kitchen towel. Apply the rub all over the meat. Place the roast in an aluminum baking pan fat side down. Place the pan in the oven and roast uncovered for 4 to 4½ hours, until the pork reaches an internal temperature of 195°F. Remove the pork from the oven, cover with aluminum foil, and let it rest for at least 30 minutes and up to 1 hour (it will continue to cook while it rests off the heat, raising the internal temperature to the desired 205°F). When it reaches 205°F, you can pull the pork, chop it, or slice it as you wish and serve it immediately, with extra sauce and buns on the side if you like.

But what's the easiest way to smoke a pork shoulder?

Here's where "knowing your cuts" really comes in handy (see page 155). Because if you know your cuts, you already know that if you want to smoke a shoulder you can just smoke part of it—the Boston blade roast or Boston butt—that decision right there makes it a quicker, easier, and cheaper cooking process. Take care, though, to never smoke a boneless pork shoulder: The bone gives the roast the stability it needs to hold together in the smoker and helps it cook more consistently with the low-heat method.

HOW DO I KEEP THE PULLED PORK FROM DRYING OUT BEFORE I SERVE IT?

To keep pulled pork from drying out, make a solution using equal parts of vinegar-based barbecue sauce (page 78) and water. For a Simple Smoked Pork Shoulder, I would use 1 cup of sauce with 1 cup of water. Pour the two ingredients into a medium saucepan and heat them over medium heat until the mixture is combined and very hot but NOT boiling. I repeat: Do not bring the mixture to a boil. When it is hot, pull it off the stove. Then, while wearing heavy-duty kitchen gloves, use your hands to toss some "half-and-half" mixture with your pulled pork, taking care to moisten as much meat as you can. This will keep your meat from drying out. You can also use the "half-and-half" technique to keep your brisket slices from drying out, too.

SIMPLE SMOKED PORK SHOULDER

SERVES 10 TO 12

ingredients

One (7½- to 10-pound) bone-in Boston butt/blade roast

1 recipe Pork Marinade (page 68)

1 cup Jack's Old South Original Rub or make your own (see page 72)

1 cup apple juice

1 cup Jack's Old South Hickory Sauce or make your own (see page 77)

Place the Boston butt in a large aluminum baking pan, add the marinade, and cover. Marinate the butt in the refrigerator for at least 2 hours, or preferably overnight.

Prepare the smoker and heat it to 300°F. Prep the shoulder: Remove the meat from the marinade and discard the marinade. Pat the meat dry all over with paper towels or a clean kitchen towel. Apply the rub all over the meat. Place it in the smoker for 2 hours. This allows the meat to absorb enough smoke to flavor it and get a good mahogany color. After two hours, remove the shoulder from the smoker and transfer it into a new clean, deep aluminum pan. Pour in the apple juice. Put the pan back in the smoker, still running at 300°F. Pull it out when the internal temperature reaches 200°F, 2 to 3 hours, with a total cook time of 4 to 4½ hours. Remove the pan from the smoker, cover it with foil, and wrap it in an old thick blanket to rest. Let the shoulder rest this way for 2 to 4 hours. Resting is as important as the cooking, as the shoulder will continue to cook when it's off the heat. When you're ready to eat, you can pull the pork, chop it, or slice it as you wish and serve it immediately, with extra sauce and buns on the side if you like.

Q:

Have you ever tried pork burgers?

A:

Does the honey badger not give a damn? (Incidentally, I love that honey badger.) If something is made of pork, rest assured that I've tried it. I do like pork burgers, although I've had some that were too dried out to be tasty. Let me tell you how you can avoid that pitfall and make yourself some delicious pork burgers: Use barbecue sauce *in* the burger. Packs in the flavor, seals in the moisture. Thank me later.

SMOKED PORK BURGERS

MAKES 2 LARGE OR 4 SMALL BURGERS

ingredients

1 pound ground pork (not too lean: at least 15% pork fat or, if you can get your pork ground for you at a butcher shop, ask for a little more)

1 yellow onion, finely diced

1 tablespoon kosher salt

1 teaspoon freshly ground black pepper

½ cup Jack's Old South Hickory Sauce or make your own (see page 77)

1 cup Classic Creamy Coleslaw (page 297)

2 or 4 onion rolls, split and toasted

Brown mustard (optional)

Sliced dill pickles (optional)

Heat a smoker to 350°F.

In a large bowl, combine the pork, diced onion, salt, pepper, and barbecue sauce. Knead to combine, but do not overwork. Form the mixture into 2 large or 4 small patties. Place the patties in an aluminum pan (either a small one for 2 burgers or a medium one for 4), and set the pan in the smoker. Smoke for about 7 minutes, or until the bottoms of the burgers begin to brown and form a crust. Remove the pan from the smoker and gently flip the burgers using a spatula. Return the pan to the smoker and smoke the burgers for 8 more minutes. Cook until an instant-read meat thermometer inserted into the side of a burger reads 160°F for medium.

Serve the burgers, topped with a scoop of coleslaw, on the prepared onion rolls, which you may slather with mustard and top with pickles if you like.

Q:

How do I smoke bologna?

A:

When somebody asks me anything about bologna, I know they're my people. This large smoked pork-based sausage is what I grew up on, eating slices of it on white bread with mustard and pickles. That is damn good, y'all. I know some folks like to put bologna down because it's a processed meat product, something considered low-class these days. I don't care much for trends: I grew up eating bologna, and I love bologna, and so did my dad, Jack. In fact, so do a lot of other professional barbecuers: At many a Memphis in May World Barbecue Championship I have spied teams cooking up smoked bologna to snack on during those long days (and nights). I have two favorite ways of cooking bologna for those enthusiasts out there who aren't afraid to admit it, and here they are.

BARBECUE BOLOGNA SANDWICHES

You might have to purchase your whole unsliced bologna from the butcher shop or butcher counter if you can't find anything but the sliced kind where you live. It's inexpensive and absolutely worth it, trust me.

ingredients

1 (3- to 5-pound) good-quality whole unsliced bologna (any kind will do, including kosher all-beef)

1 recipe Jack's Old South Hickory Rub or make your own (see page 72)

1 loaf Texas toast, sliced 1 inch thick

1 recipe Classic Creamy Coleslaw (page 297)

1 recipe Jack's Old South Hickory Sauce or make your own (see page 77)

Prepare your smoker and heat it to 225°F.

Using a sharp chef's knife, make a vertical cut that runs the length of the bologna but does not cut all the way through it: Aim to make the cut about two-thirds of the way through the bologna. Again: Be sure not to cut all the way through the bologna. Apply the rub to the bologna inside and out. Put the bologna in an aluminum pan and place the pan in the smoker. Smoke the bologna for about 3 hours, until it is mahogany in color and reaches an internal temperature of 145°F. Let the bologna rest, uncovered, for 10 minutes.

When the bologna has cooled, slice it into ½-inch-thick slices about. Place 2 slices of bologna on top of a piece of Texas toast. Top with a small scoop of slaw and a drizzle of sauce. Cover with another piece of Texas toast. Serve the sandwiches immediately.

SMOKED PEPPER JACK-STUFFED BOLOGNA SANDWICHES

SERVES 10 TO 12

I first saw barbecue cooks making and eating this at competitions, and if you make it for yourself, you'll see why it's become so beloved in my house, too.

ingredients

1 (6½-pound) good-quality whole unsliced bologna

1 pound pepper jack cheese, cut into ½-inch cubes

3 cups Jack's Old South Hickory Sauce or make your own (see page 77)

1 large loaf of crusty sourdough bread, sliced

Favorite brand of mustard, to taste

Favorite brand of hot sauce, to taste

1 sweet onion, such as Vidalia, sliced

Prepare your smoker and heat it to 250°F.

Remove the bulb end of a turkey baster. Use the opened end to core through the middle of the log of bologna. You will remove a long, thick tube of the meat. Reserve two 2-inch pieces of that tube and save the rest for another use.

Fill the open core of the bologna with the pepper jack cubes, then use the two reserved pieces of bologna to plug the ends. Put the bologna in a large aluminum pan, place it in the smoker, and smoke for 1½ hours.

Remove the pan from the smoker and glaze the bologna with the barbecue sauce. Return it to the smoker and smoke it for another 15 minutes, or until the sauce is thoroughly caramelized on the outside of the bologna.

Remove the pan from the smoker. Let the bologna rest in the pan, loosely covered, for 10 minutes.

Slice the bologna into ¾-inch slices. Place each slice on a piece of sourdough bread. Slather the meat with mustard, add a few drips of hot sauce, and top with slices of sweet onion. Cover with another slice of bread and serve immediately.

Can I smoke pork tenderloin?

I think it's worth it to fire up your smoker for just about any cut of pork because smoked pork is the most delicious stuff there is. That said, I suggest that if you want to smoke a pork tenderloin, you should consider:

— Smoking a loin, which is larger, less delicate and tender, and thus easier to smoke and more difficult to mess up

— Smoking more than one pork loin, so you have leftovers

— Also smoking something else that's small and relatively simple to smoke (like a whole chicken, for example, see page 105) so you get your time's worth out of the smoking process

SMOKED PORK LOIN

SERVES 6

Here's the best way to smoke a pork loin: This is a very easy process, and as far as smoking goes, it doesn't take much time. Pork roasts are big crowd favorites, and serving one will make you look good, too.

ingredients

1 (4½- to 5-pound) large boneless pork loin roast

1 recipe Pork Marinade (page 68)

3 cups Old South Original Rub or make your own (see page 72)

1 recipe Tangy Sweet Sauce (page 78)

Place the pork roast in a medium-size aluminum baking pan. Pour the marinade over the meat and cover the pan. Let the loin rest, covered, in the refrigerator for at least 4 hours, or preferably overnight.

When you are ready to cook the pork, heat your smoker to 350°F.

Remove the pan from the refrigerator. Remove the pork from the marinade and discard the marinade. Use paper towels or a clean kitchen towel to pat the pork dry. Coat the pork all over with the rub. Place it back in the pan, put the pan in the smoker, and smoke the pork for 1½ hours, or until its internal temperature reaches 155°F.

Remove the pork from the smoker and brush it all over with Tangy Sweet Sauce. Return it to the smoker and cook for 15 minutes more, until the sauce caramelizes.

Remove the pan from the smoker and let the loin rest, loosely covered, for 30 minutes. Cut it into ½-inch-thick slices and serve.

Can I smoke a pork belly?

For me, all the fuss about these restaurants in big cities serving up pork belly tacos and pork belly curry and stuff like that is pretty funny—I've been eating smoked pork belly all my life, so I didn't need somebody with a kitchen and an Instagram account to tell me how tasty and special it is. For a bunch of years I used to go down to the South Beach Wine & Food Festival in Miami—before my barbecue commitments made doing that pretty much impossible. It's a lot of fun to barbecue in that setting, around lots of what they call "the beautiful people" and famous chefs, too. Imagine how surprised they were when this ol' pitmaster from South Georgia showed up with pork belly sliders—the kind of trendy food those hipsters just love. Yeah, I can cook that way, too, if I want to. And so can you, from the comfort of your backyard.

SMOKED PORK BELLY SLIDERS

ingredients

1 (3-pound) pork belly side (this will likely need to be ordered from a butcher)

¼ cup Jack's Old South Hickory Sauce or make your own (see page 77)

1 recipe Classic Creamy Coleslaw (page 297)

½ English (seedless) cucumber, thinly sliced

12 to 16 small slider buns or potato rolls

Transfer the belly to a large zip-top plastic bag, pour the sauce over the top, close the bag and make sure to squeeze all the air out of it, then massage the meat with the sauce. Refrigerate for at least 4 hours, or preferably overnight.

When you are ready to smoke the belly, prepare the smoker and heat it to 275°F.

Prepare the belly for smoking: Use a sharp paring knife to score the pork belly by making a few slices in both vertical and horizontal directions across the top of it. The cuts should not be too deep or penetrating into the belly—only ¼-inch through at most. Transfer the belly to a medium-size aluminum pan. Place the pan in the smoker and smoke the belly for 3 to 4 hours, until internal temperature is 200°F. Remove the pan from the smoker and let the pork belly rest, uncovered in its pan, for 10 minutes. Using a sharp chef's knife, slice the pork belly into 1-inch-thick slices.

To assemble the sandwiches, place a slice of pork belly, a scoop of slaw, and a slice of cucumber on the bottom half of each slider bun. Top with the other half of the buns and serve immediately. Folks eat these up like they're candy.

Can I smoke a ham?

The question here is phrased wrong, people. Because not only can you smoke a ham, you sure as hell should smoke one. A ham's natural flavor is special, because that meat is sweet and mild—and if you kiss it with a little smoke, you have something that makes a Christmas dinner or an Easter brunch pretty unforgettable. But you shouldn't smoke ham only for special occasions. Get smart and smoke on any Saturday and Sunday and have sandwiches for the rest of the week.

Note: The "ham" I call for here is one that's already smoked and cured, which you should be able to find in any good grocery store. I don't tend to smoke fresh uncured hams because they turn out so much like pork shoulders—and that's a barbecue specialty. This here is more like an old-fashioned honey-baked ham with a smoky twist.

SLOW-SMOKED HAM

ingredients

1 (15-pound) precooked smoked ham on the bone

1½ cups seedless blackberry jam (apricot jam or orange marmalade can be substituted)

1 cup Dijon mustard

1 cup light brown sugar, firmly packed

½ cup Jack's Old South Hickory Rub or make your own (see page 68)

Prepare a smoker with soaked wood chips and heat it to 225°F (see page 57). Alternately, prepare a gas grill or charcoal grill for smoking and heat to medium-low heat (see page 46).

Use a sharp chef's knife to trim the ham's tough outer skin and excess fat. Place the ham meat side down in a deep aluminum baking pan. Cover the pan and smoke the ham in the prepared smoker for 2 hours without uncovering it. After 2 hours, remove the pan from the smoker.

While the ham rests, make the glaze: In a medium bowl, combine the jam, mustard, and brown sugar, stirring to combine. Uncover the ham and brush it all over with half of the glaze, reserving the remaining glaze. Cover the ham with the foil and return the pan to the smoker. Smoke the ham for about 1 hour more, or until the internal temperature reaches 145°F. Unwrap the foil and baste the ham thoroughly with the remaining glaze.

Cover the ham pan again and place it back in the smoker. Smoke, covered, for about 1 hour more. At this point the ham will be at least 145°F, or maybe a bit higher. Remove the ham from the smoker, loosely tent it with foil, and allow it to rest for 30 minutes.

Carve the ham into thin slices and serve it either warm or at room temperature.

What's the best thing to do with leftover pulled pork when I'm done eating sandwiches?

America is a country whose earliest cooks really valued thrift. I'm not talking about buying things cheap when I say "thrift," either. I'm talking about allocating your resources wisely and carefully, and not wasting what you can't use in the moment. We did not waste food in our house. And so it's no wonder I love leftovers. I start thinking about what I'm going to do with them while the meat is still cooking on the smoker. Here is one of my all-time-favorite leftover recipes.

BABY BACK MAC

Don't come up to me and tell me you never have any leftovers. I'll tell you that you're not planning right. When you fire up your smoker and make ribs, be sure to make an extra few racks—make more than you think you'll eat, so you'll have another meal (or two) after you do all that work in your smoker. Problem solved. You can substitute pulled pork, brisket, or chicken for the rib meat called for here. But nothing sounds cooler than "Baby Back Mac," which is why I chose to use rib meat for this recipe.

ingredients

4 tablespoons (½ stick) unsalted butter, softened, divided

Kosher salt, to taste

1 pound elbow macaroni

2 tablespoons all-purpose flour

3 cups whole milk (2% can be substituted, but please, no skim)

2½ cups shredded sharp cheddar cheese

Freshly ground black pepper, to taste

1 pound leftover baby back rib meat (leftover pulled pork, brisket, and pulled chicken all make good substitutions)

Use 1 tablespoon butter to grease a 13 by 9-inch baking pan all over the bottom and sides.

Bring a large heavy pot of salted water to boil over high heat. Add the macaroni and cook al dente according to package directions. When finished, drain the pasta in a colander and then rinse it under cold water to prevent it from cooking further. Set the pasta aside.

Melt the remaining butter in a medium saucepan over medium-high heat. Sprinkle the flour over the melted butter and whisk, stirring constantly for about 1 minute, until the butter and flour form a paste that is just beginning to brown. Slowly whisk in the milk, a little at time, until it's thoroughly combined with the paste. You should have a thickened milky sauce. Increase the heat while whisking the sauce until it just begins to bubble. Remove the saucepan from the heat. Whisk in 2 cups of the cheese and season with salt and pepper.

Preheat the broiler.

Pour the macaroni into the prepared baking pan. Add the cheese sauce and stir in the leftover meat. Stir to combine and evenly distribute in the pan. Scatter the remaining cheese on top. Put the pan in the broiler and cook until the cheese begins to brown and bubble, 4 to 5 minutes. Remove from the broiler, cover with foil, and let stand for 10 minutes. Serve and enjoy.

BARBECUE-STUFFED BAKED POTATOES

At my dad's take-out barbecue restaurant here in South Georgia, he thought to put barbecue-stuffed baked potatoes on the menu as a way to use up any leftovers of meat we had on hand but couldn't or didn't sell by the pound or the platter. It was smart and it was popular—our customers loved these and ordered them all the time, and my brother and I still crave these and make them all the time, too.

ingredients

4 large Idaho baking potatoes (about 12 ounces each)

2 tablespoons olive oil

Kosher salt, to taste

1 cup sour cream (plus more for garnish)

5 tablespoons unsalted butter, at room temperature

Freshly ground black pepper, to taste

1 pound leftover pulled pork (see page 162)

1 cup shredded sharp cheddar cheese

4 tablespoons chopped green onions (scallions), white and tender green parts only

Preheat the oven to 425°F.

Rinse the potatoes well under cool water and scrub them clean. Dry them thoroughly with paper towels or a clean kitchen towel. Using a fork, pierce each potato all over on both sides (this creates vents that allow steam to escape from the potatoes while they cook—you need to do this to ensure the potato doesn't explode). Pour the olive oil into a shallow baking dish and roll the potatoes in it to coat the skins. Sprinkle the potatoes all over with salt. Transfer to a baking pan. Bake the potatoes directly on the oven rack until they are very soft when squeezed and the skins are crisp, 50 to 60 minutes. Let cool just until you can hold them.

Using a serrated knife, slice the potatoes in half lengthwise and, leaving enough flesh on the skin so the shells remain intact, scoop the flesh into a medium bowl. Transfer the shells to a rimmed baking sheet. Combine the scooped potato with the sour cream, butter, and salt and pepper and mash with a fork until well combined and smooth. Fold in the leftover pulled pork and ½ cup of the cheese.

Increase the oven temperature to 450°F. Spoon the mixture into the reserved potato skins. Bake until the filling is puffed and browned in spots, about 20 minutes. Remove the potatoes from the oven, top with the remaining cheese and the green onions (and some fresh cold sour cream, if you like) and serve immediately.

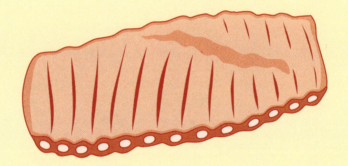

HANDLING IT

ALL ABOUT COOKING RIBS & CHOPS

Championship
St. Louis Ribs
page 189

Peach
Baked Beans
page 301

Potato Salad
page 299

what's better: pork ribs or beef ribs?

If the South had to be summed up in just one food, there are a lot of good contenders—pimiento cheese, deviled eggs, and biscuits, to list a few. But for most folks, let's face it: The South is rib country. Ain't no doubt about it. Whole hog may mean "barbecue" for professionals like me, but regular folks sitting on sofas at home? Their favorite is ribs. Believe me, I see people on the hunt for ribs at every competition. And they're talking about pork ribs. It's not that beef ribs aren't as tasty—they are. In fact, some of my fellow barbecue competitors even prefer to cook, when the rules allow it, those big honking beef bones—they call them "dinosaur bones"—over the smaller, thinner pork ribs. Those people are generally not from around here in South Georgia. They're in Texas (where beef rules) or up North. But I learned to make ribs because of competitions. They weren't what I ate at home. We ate pork shoulders, because they were cheap and plentiful.

In the world of professional barbecue, you cannot underestimate how important the category of ribs is. It's the only category of meat you can compete in to win in both of the sanctioning barbecue contest organizations—the Kansas City Barbecue Society (KCBS) and the Memphis Barbecue Network (MBN). The KCBS allows beef and other meats, but MBN is a hog-only contest. Ribs, however, are important in both. What judges look for in a winning rib, be it pork or beef, is the following:

Ribs should be, above all, soft—by that I mean soft to bite into, so that you don't have to tear away the meat with your teeth or bite down so hard on the sucker that you worry about your gums. It should be soft but not mushy—you want the texture of your ribs to hold together enough that they don't disintegrate.

PORK RIBS & CHOPS

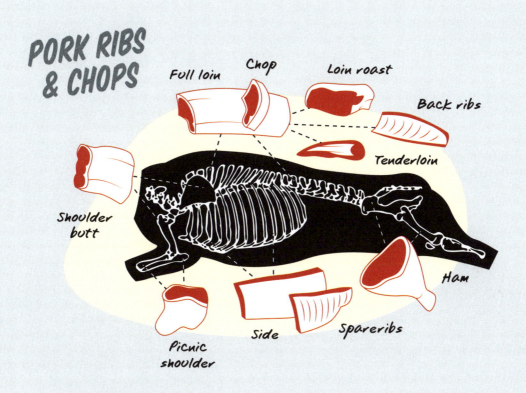

Full loin · Chop · Loin roast · Back ribs · Tenderloin · Shoulder butt · Ham · Picnic shoulder · Side · Spareribs

BEEF RIBS & CHOPS

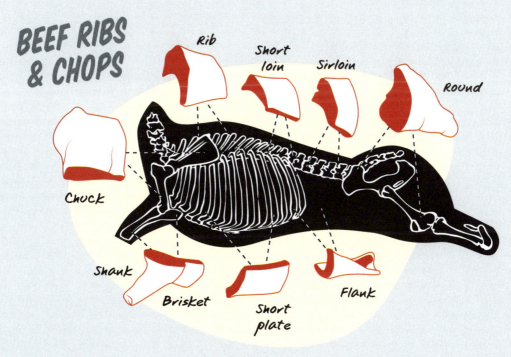

Rib · Short loin · Sirloin · Round · Chuck · Shank · Brisket · Short plate · Flank

You want them to taste smoky, but not too smoky—they should always have a little touch of sweetness to them to balance the intensity of the smoke. Finally, you want your ribs to be shiny, to gleam in the sunshine and not look like little black lumps. Not sure how to do all that? Stay with me in this chapter and I'll teach you. I'll even teach you how to cook beef ribs, too.

MYRON MIXON'S RIB THEORY

Y'all know how Oprah always talks about one thing she knows is true? Don't act like you haven't seen her book *What I Know for Sure* or read any of her "What I Know for Sure" columns. Even I have. Here's one thing *I* know for sure: People like to eat food that they can pick up and carry, that they don't need a knife and fork or even a plate in order to enjoy. I'm talking about foods with built-in handles: corn dogs, sliders, tacos, chicken wings, turkey legs . . . and, of course, ribs. It's so convenient to have a food you can grip and eat without having to even sit down. Look at the success of all those food trucks if you don't believe me. Go to any barbecue competition and you'll see people walking around waiting for the ribs and then walking around with ribs in their hands.

RIB BUYING TIPS

For St. Louis ribs: A slab weighs 2 to 3 pounds (smaller usually means more tender) and will feed two or three people.

For baby backs: A slab weighs 1 to 2 pounds, has at least 8 ribs, and most rib lovers are good for a whole slab to themselves.

Note that in both cases about half the weight of the slab is bone, and then you won't have to feel too bad about how many you eat.

For all ribs: Look for a good ratio of meat to fat. Don't be afraid of the fat: Those striations of fat running near the bone provide flavor and keep the meat moist while you cook.

As all folks who buy meat advise: Think pink. That pure pinkish red color signifies healthy meat. Do not buy dry-looking or grayish ribs, or ribs that have dark spots on the fat portions. (That holds true for any kind of meat, for that matter.)

Do smell the package: If you can smell the meat through it, put it down. It should be odorless. (This holds true for any kind of meat, too.)

Avoid shiners. That's what we call the bones that break through the meat on the front or back of a rack. That bone is going to burn and then dry out the ribs near it.

It's best to cook spareribs soon after buying them, although racks of ribs can be stored in the fridge for up to three days. Any longer than three days and you ought to freeze them; they will keep for up to six months. To thaw: Give frozen ribs roughly 12 to 14 hours to thaw in the refrigerator before cooking.

Q:

What are ribs, anyway?

A:

It's extremely useful to know where your ribs come from, because that'll give you some clues as to how best to cook them. Take a look:

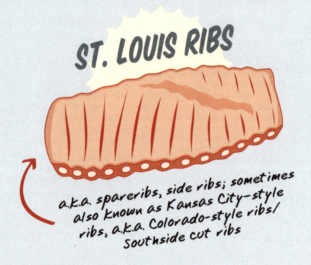

ST. LOUIS RIBS

a.k.a. spareribs, side ribs; sometimes also known as Kansas City-style ribs, a.k.a. Colorado-style ribs/ Southside cut ribs

St. Louis ribs are cut from the belly of the hog, especially from the lower part behind the hog's shoulder and breastbone. From there, butchers trim off the breastbone (sternum) and skirt (chewy belly cartilage). What remains: Ribs that are long and straight, both flatter and fattier than baby back ribs. I mean that last part in a good way—that fat is good for smoking and it makes the ribs taste good, too. The result is a uniformly trimmed squared-up rack of spareribs, a meaty rectangle of meat and bone with very little fat left on it. These are most likely what you see at restaurants and competitions, simply because they look better—the most cleaned-up version of a sparerib.

COUNTRY-STYLE RIBS

Country-style ribs are cut from the blade end of the pig, close to the shoulder. The bone is almost always removed and they're sold boneless, so note that they contain no actual rib bones (if you see bone in there, it's from the shoulder blade). It's always confused me as to why these are called "ribs" when "blade-end pork chops" might be a better and more truthful name. Regardless, I don't cook them much because even though they're meaty as hell, they turn mushy quickly—not a good idea for smoking, where you need a cut that is sturdier and holds together. But they're good for Crock-Pots and stews.

Baby back ribs come from the top of the hog's rib cage, between the hog's spine and the spareribs. They are short (hence the "baby"), curved, and often meatier than spareribs. One rack averages 10 to 13 ribs, each one anywhere from 3 to 6 inches long. They're both more tender and leaner than spareribs, and thus more in demand—and of course, more expensive. Most folks on Earth—at least the ones who eat meat—love 'em.

BABY BACK RIBS

a.k.a. back ribs, loin ribs, or pork loin back ribs

RIBLETS

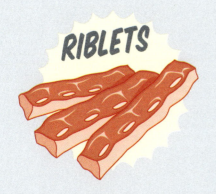

Riblets are the curved tips from pork spareribs that are sometimes cut in order to straighten them out—to get that squared-off St. Louis cut, in particular. To do this, the full set of spareribs are cut with a bone saw. What you have then on one side is your St. Louis ribs, and on the other you have these short, flat ribs, with the curved part removed. Sometimes riblets are incorrectly referred to as "rib tips," but these are actually different cuts of pork. Riblets are just another cut from spareribs that taste great smoked.

How do I make great pork ribs?

You want to make my world championship–winning St. Louis ribs? You're going to need to do some planning and some rereading to get started. Creating a deep and rich flavor profile is especially important for making delicious ribs. This starts with meat prep and marinade, continues with a rub, expands with a spritz, and finally ends with a glaze. Go back and check out my thoughts on how to build a great flavor profile before you set out on your rib journey (page 64). Then devote some time to thinking through each stage: Your marinade should be on point, your rub should be applied correctly, your spritz should be judiciously timed, and you should understand and master the role of the glaze in the cooking process. Ribs are deceptively simple: They look small and cute and thus seem easy to prepare, but getting them to taste just right is a much bigger effort. Don't worry, you can do it. I figured it out, and so can you.

CHAMPIONSHIP ST. LOUIS RIBS

SERVES 8 TO 12

I recommend cooking four racks of ribs, which should be enough to serve 8 hungry rib lovers or 12 rib pickers who'll be eating a lot of side dishes alongside the ribs. If you're going to cook fewer ribs, you'll still need to make the rub, marinade, and glaze, so my thought is: Make more ribs than you need. You can save those leftovers and thank me later. Note that regardless of how many racks of ribs you're cooking, the cook time stays the same.

ingredients

4 racks spareribs

1 recipe Rib Marinade (page 69)

3 cups Jack's Old South Original Rub or make your own (see page 72)

1 recipe Rib Spritz (page 191)

1 cup apple juice

1 recipe Pork Glaze (page 75)

tools

2 solid cutting boards

1 sharp boning knife or paring knife

Myron Mixon Rib Skinner (or clean kitchen towels)

3 to 4 aluminum baking pans

Aluminum foil

1 medium-size plastic spray bottle

1 brush to apply glaze

One at a time, place the slabs of spareribs on the cutting board, bone-side down. Trim off the excess fat, especially around the first three ribs. Turn the slab over so that now it's bone side up. There's a clear thick membrane covering and connecting the bones (called "the silver," which butchers and even some grocery stores might remove for you), and you'll need to remove this because it prevents rubs and sauces from adhering to the rib meat, and you want those flavors on your ribs. Use your sharp knife to slide it under the silver. Once you have penetrated the silver with a knife, work your fingers underneath it until you have 2 to 3 inches cleared. Use your Myron Mixon Rib Skinner (or a clean kitchen towel) to grab the membrane and then gently yet firmly pull the membrane all the way off the rack of ribs. Discard the membrane. Pulling off the membrane will expose loose fat on the ribs that you can trim off with your paring knife. Repeat this process with all the racks.

Now that you've prepped your racks, you need to do the St. Louis cut—this ensures that the ribs will be as uniform in size as they can be, which is important for your cook time and doneness. Pick the longest bone near the breastbone and use it as a guideline of where to make the horizontal cut along the length of the slab, so you can separate the ribs from the breastbone. Cut all the way across the rack to separate the

recipe continues

smaller curved ribs from the long ones. You should end up with two slabs of ribs that are 5 to 6 inches in length. Reserve the shorter part to make riblets—refrigerate them in an aluminum pan until ready to cook.

After the ribs are properly trimmed, set the racks in a deep aluminum baking pan. Cover the ribs with the rib marinade. Cover the pan with aluminum foil and let it sit for 4 hours, either in the refrigerator or, if you're at a contest or in a picnic situation, in a cooler packed with ice.

When you are ready to smoke the ribs, remove them from the marinade. Pat the ribs dry with clean kitchen towels or paper towels. Apply the rub to the ribs lightly, around the edges of the ribs and over the backside of them, and on top. Then let the ribs sit, uncovered, at room temperature for 30 minutes.

In the meantime, heat your smoker to 275°F. Transfer the ribs to a clean aluminum baking pan. When the smoker is ready, put the pan of ribs in the smoker. Close the smoker and smoke the ribs for 3 hours. After the first 45 minutes, open the smoker and spritz the ribs all over with the rib spritz. Close the smoker and continue to spritz the ribs in this manner in 15-minute intervals, until the 3 hours is up.

Remove the rib pan from the smoker. Pour the apple juice into a clean aluminum baking pan. Place the ribs in the pan, bone side down, and cover the pan with aluminum foil. Place the pan in the smoker and smoke for 2 hours.

Remove the pan from the smoker and shut off the heat in the smoker. Remove the foil from the pan and apply the pork glaze to the tops and bottoms of the racks of ribs. Cover the pan with the foil again, return it to the smoker, and let the ribs rest in the smoker for 1 hour as the temperature in the smoker gradually drops.

After an hour resting in the smoker, remove the pan from the smoker and transfer the rib racks to a clean cutting board. Let the ribs rest for 10 minutes, then cut them to separate them and serve immediately.

RIB SPRITZ

This is what I use on pork ribs. It's an added step that will improve the look and taste of your ribs. Make it the day before if you need to or do it right after you put your ribs on the smoker, and then start spritzing after your ribs have been on the smoker for 45 minutes.

3 cups apple juice

2 cups white wine vinegar

2 tablespoons liquid imitation butter

In a large spray bottle (one that will hold at least 5 cups of liquid), combine all the ingredients. Shake well to blend.

WHY DO YOU SPRITZ YOUR RIBS?

Y'all ask me this question so often it's like you've never seen one of those fancy chefs on *Top Chef* or whatever you watch spritzing food before. I spritz my ribs for the same reason those folks spritz whatever they're cooking: because it's a technique I like, and I like it in this case it because it keeps the back of the ribs moist during the smoking time and also adds another layer of flavor to the ribs. People sometimes look at me funny when they see me doing it, but do you think I care? Rest assured that I have not even one chicken bone of concern about that. And people look at me even funnier when they see that I use imitation butter—which comes in the kind of small plastic bottle that vanilla extract comes in—that I found in the spice section of supermarkets. Again, I don't care, because I have a good reason for doing that: Melted "real" butter is still too thick to get through a spray bottle. To my health nuts out there: Don't worry, one ounce of the imitation stuff, which is just soybean oil, will not kill you. To spritz properly, here's the deal: You must get the color on the ribs just right before you start spritzing—or else you're going to end up washing your bark off with the spritz. That's why I've got this process timed the way it is.

Q:

How do I make baby back ribs?

A:

Now it can be told: My favorite ribs to cook *and* eat are baby backs. They're the rib of choice for MBN contests, which I've done so well at over the years—so they're kind of a sentimental favorite, too. Over the years I've developed a real love for them because I had to work hard to perfect my baby back technique, and they've won me a hell of a lot of money. And here it is, for free, for you. Well, almost for free. But this recipe alone is worth the price of this book, I promise you.

BABY BACK RIBS

SERVES 4 TO 6

ingredients

4 racks baby back ribs

1 recipe Rib Marinade
(page 69)

3 cups Jack's Old South
Original Rub or make your
own (see page 72)

1 recipe Rib Spritz
(page 191)

1 cup apple juice

1 recipe Pork Glaze
(page 75)

tools

1 solid cutting board

1 sharp paring knife or
boning knife

Myron Mixon Rib Skinner
(or clean kitchen towel)

3 to 4 aluminum baking pans

1 brush to apply glaze

One at a time, place the racks on a cutting board, bone side up, and remove the membrane (or "silver") from the back of the ribs, if it hasn't already been removed. You need to remove this because it prevents rubs and sauces from adhering to the rib meat, and you want those flavors on your ribs. Once you have penetrated the silver with a knife, work your fingers underneath it until you have 2 to 3 inches cleared. Use your Myron Mixon Rib Skinner (or a kitchen towel) to grab the membrane and then gently yet firmly pull the membrane all the way off the rack of ribs. Discard the membrane. Pulling off the membrane will expose loose fat on the ribs that you can trim off with your paring knife. Repeat this process with all the racks.

Set the racks in an aluminum baking pan and cover them completely with the Rib Marinade. Cover the pan with aluminum foil and let sit for 4 hours, either in the refrigerator or, if you're in a contest or picnic situation, in a cooler packed with ice.

When you are ready to cook them, remove the ribs from the marinade. Pat them dry with towels. Apply the rub lightly around the edges of the ribs, over the back side of them, and on top. Then let the ribs sit, uncovered, at room temperature for 30 minutes.

In the meantime, heat the smoker to 250°F.

Transfer the ribs to the baking pan, put the pan in the smoker, and smoke for 2 hours. After the first 30 minutes of smoking, spritz the ribs with the Rib Spritz. Continue to spritz in 15-minute intervals for the duration of the cook time.

recipe continues

After 2 hours, remove the pan from the smoker. Pour the apple juice into a clean aluminum baking pan. Place the ribs in the pan, bone-side down, and cover the pan with aluminum foil. Place the pan back in the smoker and smoke for 1 hour.

Remove the pan from the smoker and shut off the heat on the smoker. Remove the foil from the rib pan and apply the glaze to the top and bottom of the slabs of ribs. Cover the pan with the foil again, return it to the smoker, and let the ribs rest in the smoker for 30 minutes as the temperature gradually drops.

After 30 minutes, remove the ribs from the smoker, uncover them, and let them rest for 10 minutes on a clean cutting board. Then cut them to separate them and serve immediately.

How do I make beef ribs?

You can smoke short ribs or long ribs—those back ribs that look like dinosaur bones—with equally great results. I'm giving you a method you can use for both. In the supermarket, finding short ribs is probably easier than long ribs—but if you can't find the longer back ribs, you can ask a butcher to order them for you. These ribs are not only big but also tender and succulent; that's because the rib roast, a prime cut of meat, sits directly above them. That makes them prime, too—imagine a prime rib on a stick and you've got the idea. So, you don't want to screw these up when you cook them. The cooking method is similar to what I use for baby back ribs, but I don't marinate beef ribs in liquid: You don't need to, since they're already so well marbled. But I do season them and let them sit in a rub overnight, which I've found really brings out their natural rich flavor.

SMOKED BEEF RIBS

SERVES 4

ingredients

7½ to 8 pounds beef short ribs or whole beef ribs (also known as beef plate ribs); this should guarantee at least 3 ribs per person

2 tablespoons kosher salt

2 tablespoons freshly ground black pepper

3 tablespoons dark brown sugar

2 teaspoons chili powder

1 teaspoon ground turmeric

1 teaspoon ground coriander

1 teaspoon garlic powder

1 teaspoon onion powder

1 recipe Tangy Sweet Sauce (page 78)

tools

1 solid cutting board

1 sharp boning or paring knife

Myron Mixon Rib Skinner (or clean kitchen towel)

1 medium-size bowl

1 aluminum baking pan

1 brush to apply sauce

Place the racks on a cutting board, bone side up, and remove the membrane (or "silver") from the back of the ribs. As with pork ribs, you need to remove this because it prevents rubs and sauces from adhering to the rib meat, and you want those flavors on your ribs. Once you have penetrated the silver with a knife, work your fingers underneath it until you have 2 to 3 inches cleared. Use your Myron Mixon Rib Skinner (or a kitchen towel) to grab the membrane and then gently yet firmly pull the membrane all the way off the rack of ribs. Discard the membrane. Pulling off the membrane will expose loose fat on the ribs that you can trim off with your paring knife.

In a medium bowl, combine the salt, pepper, brown sugar, chili powder, turmeric, coriander, garlic powder, and onion powder to form a rub. Coat both sides of each rib with the spice mixture. Place the ribs in a large aluminum baking pan, cover with foil, and refrigerate overnight.

When you are ready to smoke the ribs, heat a smoker to 275°F.

Place the ribs in the smoker and smoke, uncovered, for 2 hours.

Remove the pan from the smoker and pour 2 cups of water into the pan. Cover the pan with aluminum foil, return it to the smoker, and smoke for 2 more hours.

After 2 hours, remove the ribs from the smoker. Glaze the tops (front side) of the ribs only with the Tangy Sweet Sauce. Don't overdo it with too much sauce: Use just enough to coat the ribs. Put the pan back in the smoker and smoke the ribs, uncovered, for 15 minutes.

Remove the pan from the smoker. Transfer the ribs to a cutting board and let them rest, loosely covered with aluminum foil, for 10 minutes. Cut the ribs to separate them and eat them immediately.

Q:

What's the easiest way to make ribs?

A:

People are always looking for shortcuts when it comes to cooking barbecue, and I think it's because they don't like being patient with how long the process of smoking sometimes takes. Spareribs are a good place to find shortcuts: You can easily have a butcher trim those suckers up for you. It'll cost you a little more, but it'll also save you some time. Ask your butcher for St. Louis–style spareribs trimmed as uniformly as possible and with the membrane removed. And you can skip the spritzing process, too—that's a helpful and nice extra touch, but you can do fine in your backyard without it, especially if you're in a hurry or are just impatient.

EASY BACKYARD SPARERIBS

SERVES 8 TO 10

ingredients

4 racks St. Louis–style spareribs

1 recipe Rib Marinade (page 69)

3 cups Jack's Old South Original Rub or make your own (see page 72)

Approximately 1 cup water

1 recipe Jack's Old South Hickory Sauce or make your own (see page 77)

Make sure your ribs are trimmed of all fat and are as uniform as possible in length, which you should've asked your butcher to do for you already. There should be no "silver" membrane on the back of them, either.

Set the racks of ribs in an aluminum baking pan and cover them completely with the marinade. Cover the pan with aluminum foil and refrigerate for at least 4 hours, or overnight.

When you are ready to cook the ribs, remove them from the marinade. Pat them dry with paper towels. Apply the rub lightly around the edges of the ribs, over the backs of them, and all over the tops. Then let the ribs sit uncovered at room temperature for at least 30 minutes, preferably 1 hour.

Prepare your smoker and heat it to 275°F.

Transfer the ribs to a clean aluminum baking pan. Put the pan in the smoker and smoke the ribs for 3 hours.

After 3 hours, remove the pan from the smoker. Pour about a cup of water into a clean aluminum baking pan. Place the ribs in the new pan, bone side down, and cover the pan with aluminum foil. Place the pan in the smoker and smoke the ribs for 2 hours.

Remove the pan from the smoker and shut off the heat in the smoker. Remove the foil from the rib pan and apply the sauce to the front and back of the slabs. Cover the pan with the foil again, return it to the smoker, and let the ribs rest in the smoker as the smoker's heat dies down, for 1 hour.

Remove the ribs from the pan and transfer them to a clean cutting board. Let the ribs rest for 10 minutes, uncovered. Cut the ribs to separate them, then serve immediately.

Can I make good ribs in the oven?

Yes. Yes, you can. It rains sometimes down here in South Georgia, too, and then I don't want to get off the couch. And even when it doesn't rain, there are times when I still don't want to get off the couch. Here's what to do:

OVEN-BAKED BARBECUE RIBS

SERVES 6

ingredients

5 pounds pork spareribs or baby back ribs, about 4 racks of St. Louis ribs, or about 6 racks of baby back ribs

¼ cup apple cider vinegar

3 cups Jack's Old South Original Rub or make your own (see page 72)

1 cup Jack's Old South Hickory Sauce or make your own (see page 77)

tools

1 solid cutting board

1 baking sheet

1 wire cooling rack

Myron Mixon Rib Skinner (or clean kitchen towels)

1 brush to apply sauce

1 sharp boning or paring knife

Preheat the oven broiler. Place an oven rack a few inches below the heating element.

Place the racks on a cutting board, bone side up, and remove the membrane (or "silver") from the back of the ribs. Penetrate the silver with a knife, then work your fingers underneath it until you have 2 to 3 inches cleared. Use a kitchen towel to grab the membrane and then gently yet firmly pull the membrane all the way off the rack of ribs. Discard the membrane.

Rub the ribs with the vinegar all over and on both sides. Pat racks dry with paper towels or a clean kitchen towel. Sprinkle the ribs with the rub.

Line a baking sheet with foil and set a cooling rack on top. Lay the ribs on top of the rack in a single layer. Make sure the meaty side of the ribs is facing up.

Broil the ribs for about 5 minutes, until the rub is bubbling and caramelizes into an even brown coating. Remove the baking sheet of ribs from the oven.

Decrease oven temperature to 300°F. When the temperature is lowered, return the baking sheet of ribs to the oven. Roast for 2½ to 3 hours for spareribs or 1½ to 2 hours for baby back ribs. Halfway through cooking, cover the ribs with aluminum foil to protect them from drying out.

About 30 minutes before the end of cooking, brush the ribs with barbecue sauce, cover with the foil again, and finish cooking.

The ribs are done when a knife slides easily into the thickest part of the rib meat. Remove the ribs from the oven and let them rest, covered, for about 15 minutes. Cut between the bones to separate the individual ribs. Serve immediately with extra barbecue sauce for dipping, if you like.

Q:

How do I smoke pork chops?

A:

Smoking pork chops is a great idea, but know that if you do it, it's best to get chops that are at least one inch thick and on the bone. The meatier the better. You want pork chops that are going to be sturdy enough to withstand the low-and-slow smoking method, not thinner chops that you'd be better off grilling hot and fast.

SMOKED PORK CHOPS

SERVES 4

ingredients

4 bone-in pork chops, at least 1 inch thick, at least 10 ounces apiece

1 cup Jack's Old South Original Rub or make your own (see page 72)

1 recipe Pork Glaze (page 75)

Sprinkle the chops with the rub all over the sides, front, and back, and pat gently to make sure the rub adheres to the meat. Transfer the chops to an aluminum baking pan and let sit with the rub for 30 minutes.

Prepare your smoker and heat it to 300°F.

Transfer the pan with the chops to the smoker when it is ready and smoke the pork chops for 1 hour. After an hour, remove the pan from the smoker and brush the pork glaze all over the chops on the front, back, and sides. Place the pan back in the smoker and smoke the chops for an additional hour, or until the internal temperature reaches 145°F on an instant-read thermometer.

Remove the pork chops from the smoker and transfer them to a wooden cutting board. Cover them loosely with foil and let them rest for 30 minutes before serving.

How do I smoke a pork roast?

To me, a pork roast is almost always a good idea, especially if you're having a few friends or family members over, because they are such crowd-pleasers. Smoking a pork roast is a very easy thing to do, almost as easy as putting one in the oven to roast, but the flavor of that smoke-kissed meat is so much richer and tastier. Just know that although you can smoke one of the smaller, leaner pork tenderloins, I recommend that you smoke a larger and denser pork loin—it's less likely to dry out in the smoker—and a pork rib roast (or a center-cut rib roast, which is the pork equivalent of prime rib) is even better because it's on the bone.

SMOKED CROWN OF PORK

SERVES 10 TO 12

ingredients

1 crown roast of pork (about 10 pounds)

1 recipe Pork Marinade (page 68)

3 cups Jack's Old South Original Rub or make your own (see page 72)

1 recipe Tangy Sweet Sauce (page 78)

The day before you plan to serve your roast, submerge the pork roast in the marinade and allow it to marinate in the refrigerator overnight, or for at least 12 hours.

When you are ready to cook the pork, heat a smoker to 350°F.

Remove the pan from the refrigerator and pat the roast dry all over with paper towels or a clean kitchen towel. Coat the roast all over the outside with the rub and transfer it to a clean aluminum pan. Place the pan in the smoker and smoke for 3 hours, or until the internal temperature reaches 155°F.

Remove the pan from the smoker and brush the Tangy Sweet Sauce all over the pork. Return the pan to the smoker and smoke the roast for 15 additional minutes. Remove the roast from the smoker and let it rest at least 20 minutes before carving. The roast will carve easily into individual chops by cutting between the bones along the angle of the bone.

How do I smoke a rack of lamb?

If you think an old South Georgia boy like me wouldn't know diddlysquat about mutton, you'd be mostly right. We don't see a whole lot of it and we don't eat it much. But if you're going to be serious about competitive barbecue, and competing in Kansas City Barbecue Society events in particular, you'll need to learn how to do this. This is doubly true if you ever plan to cook barbecue in Kentucky, where mutton is a specialty, and triply true at the International Barbecue Festival in the town of Owensboro, where mutton is *the* star attraction (they even refer to the contest's mascot as the "mutton glutton").

SMOKED RACK OF LAMB

SERVES 8

The first mutton contest I ever entered I won, and here's how I cooked the lamb chops, just like this here. Note: I like to get the largest rack of lamb I can find, so I can get chops that are at least 1-inch thick apiece. Gives people something to sink their teeth into.

ingredients

4 (1- to 1½-pound) racks of lamb, trimmed by all but ¼-inch layer of fat and frenched; each rack should have 8 ribs

2 cups dry red wine

½ cup Worcestershire sauce

2 tablespoons white vinegar

1 tablespoon kosher salt

2 tablespoons sugar

3 cups Jack's Old South Original Rub or make your own (see page 72)

1 recipe Tangy Sweet Sauce (page 78)

In a large deep aluminum baking pan, combine the red wine, Worcestershire sauce, white vinegar, salt, and sugar. Submerge the racks of lamb in the mixture and marinate them, covered, in the refrigerator overnight.

When you are ready to cook the lamb, heat your smoker to 225°F.

Remove the lamb from the marinade and discard the marinade. Season each rack lightly with the rub. (You're seasoning them lightly so the ribs don't become overly salty.) Transfer the racks to a clean aluminum baking pan, place the pan in the smoker, and smoke for 2 to 2½ hours, or until internal temperature is 135°F.

Remove the pan from the smoker and use a brush to glaze the racks with the Tangy Sweet Sauce. Put the pan back into the smoker and smoke the racks for an additional 5 minutes. Remove the pan from the smoker, transfer the racks to a wooden cutting board, and let the lamb rest, uncovered, for 15 minutes. Then slice your chops and serve them up immediately.

Can I make my own rib sandwich?

You're talking about that fast-food dish where a boneless, saucy rack of ribs is sandwiched on a bun with pickles and onions? I can tell you how to make the best damn version of that in the world. It's so good I call it The King Rib. Because I'm the King of 'Cue. These are seriously delicious—a real treat.

Here's the one thing you need to do in advance: The next time you make smoked ribs, either St. Louis Ribs or Baby Backs (see page 189 and page 193, respectively), make one extra rack. Take that rack off the smoker, let it cool to room temperature, wrap it in foil, and refrigerate it. You have three days from that time to make this sandwich.

THE KING RIB SANDWICH

ingredients

1 precooked rack of St. Louis or baby back ribs

1 cup Jack's Old South Hickory Sauce or make your own (see page 77)

4 (6-inch) sandwich rolls or buns, each split in half

1½ tablespoons unsalted butter, for buns

8 dill pickle spears or slices

½ cup finely chopped sweet onion, such as Vidalia

Unwrap your reserved slab of ribs and transfer it to a cutting board. Using a very sharp long chef's knife, you want to cut a wide horizontal slice across the whole rack. You will be left with two very long uninterrupted slices of boneless rib meat.

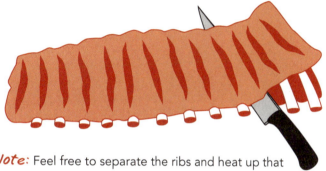

Note: Feel free to separate the ribs and heat up that in-between meat for a treat.

Once you have your two long slices of boneless rib meat, cut each in half. Now you're ready to make your sandwiches.

Preheat the oven to 350°F.

Line a baking sheet with aluminum foil. Arrange your rib meat slices on the sheet. Use a brush to glaze them all over on both sides with the sauce. You want them to be quite saucy on both sides. Transfer the baking sheet to the oven and warm up the saucy rib slabs thoroughly, about 15 to 20 minutes.

In the meantime, lightly toast and lightly butter the buns or rolls.

When the rib slabs are thoroughly warmed, lay one slab on the bottom of each roll. Arrange 2 spears or slices of pickles on top of the pork. Scatter two tablespoons of chopped onions on top of each sandwich. Cover with the top of the roll. Serve immediately, or if you like that "fast-food" feeling, microwave the sandwiches for 15 seconds on high. Then sit back and bask in your compliments.

CHAPTER SEVEN

HERE IS THE BEEF

ALL ABOUT COOKING THE COW

Myron Mixon's Brisket
page 223

Cornbread
page 306

Peach
Baked Beans
page 301

BEEF CUTS

MYRON'S THOUGHTS ON BEEF

I'm known for cooking pigs. I've won my fair share of contests by cooking whole hogs, and, of course, pork shoulders, and ribs. I grew up cooking pork at a homemade masonry pit in my childhood backyard with my dad and my brother, Tracy. Smoking pork in pits was how we made our living and how we fed our family. And in a way, I'm still doing that today. It's what we do in South Georgia. But over in Texas, they cook something that, until I became a competitive pitmaster, was totally foreign to me: brisket.

Where I'm from, steaks are for celebrations and hamburgers are the most common way we eat beef—when I was growing up, and still today. Hell, I didn't even hear the term "brisket" until I got to a barbecue contest—and then I was nervous when I realized I wasn't going to win any championships unless I figured out how to cook one. And you'd better believe that with the incentive of winning and money on the line, I learned how to cook a damn good brisket. I have my own way of doing it—hot and fast—and that's what you'll learn from me here. A lot of barbecue guys will give you a song and dance about how you have to spend a lot of time cooking a brisket, but take it from me: I had to learn how to do this from scratch, and I know that you don't need to do it that way. And you sure don't need the song and dance—or the tight jeans and tattoos—to make a great smoked brisket.

This chapter will cover my world-famous brisket, but that ain't all. I'm also going to get into nearly everything else beef-related that you're likely to want to cook in your smoker—from burgers to meatloaf (yeah, meatloaf—wait till you try it). And along the way, I'm going to talk to you like you're enrolled in one of my cooking schools: I'll explain everything from the different cuts of beef for smoking, to getting the best meat possible, to cooking it the right way (or at least my way); and I'll tell you how to deal with the pitfalls that real pitmasters encounter as you make your way to beefy barbecue perfection.

what is a brisket?

Plain and simple, a brisket is a cut of beef. It comes from the cow's shoulder and its first few ribs. On its own, it's dense and tough and stringy, and it can be difficult to figure out how to cook: How are you gonna break down those fibrous strands and get something delicious?

In the world of professional barbecuing, a brisket is a very important cut indeed—it's the *only* cut of beef that is judged for major awards and prize money at both sanctioning bodies' contests. Cooking brisket is one of the main jobs of serious barbecue competitors. Now, brisket is special to me because it's something I actually had to learn to smoke. So when I first began encountering it as I went to different barbecue contests, it was a real curiosity to me. Brisket has become one of my favorite things in the world to prepare.

It's important for you to read this before you start cooking a brisket. The more you understand about what you're trying to cook, and the more you plan in advance for how you want it to come out before you start cooking, the better.

Here's how a brisket works: A whole brisket averages about 12 pounds. You're probably used to seeing briskets in the meat case at supermarkets or in butcher shops that have already been broken down into two sub-cuts: the first, the "flat" cut, comes from closer to the cow's belly and is more evenly shaped and lean; the second, the "point" cut, comes from near the foreshank and is rounder and fattier but has more flavor. I'm going to give you a recipe for a whole untrimmed brisket, which is what I cook in competition, and which you may need to order specially from your butcher—but don't worry, it'll be worth it (page 223). If you can't get a whole untrimmed brisket or are just convinced you don't want to cook that much meat, you'll end up with a flat cut or a point; either will weigh between 4 and 8 pounds, and I'll give you a plan for how to cook that, too (page 235).

WHERE TO FIND THE BRISKET

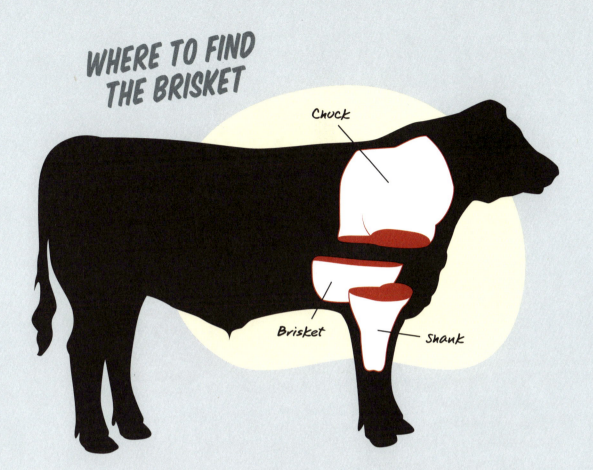

Chuck

Brisket

Shank

ANATOMY OF A BRISKET

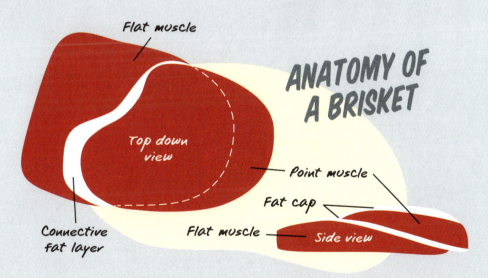

Flat muscle

Top down view

Connective fat layer

Point muscle

Fat cap

Flat muscle

Side view

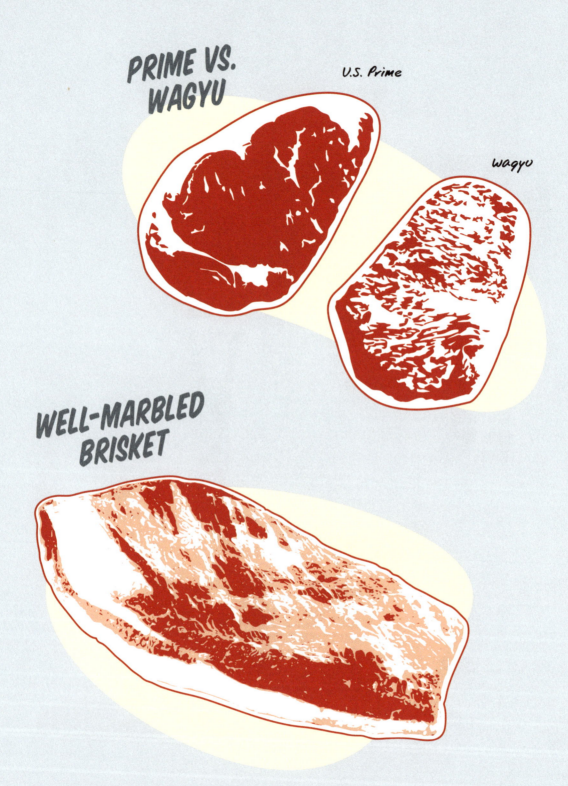

PRIME VS.
WAGYU

U.S. Prime

Wagyu

WELL-MARBLED
BRISKET

Q:

What kind of brisket should I buy?

A:

No. 1 Rule of Thumb for a Great Brisket: **To make a great brisket, you have to start with a great piece of meat. I like wagyu beef, which comes from a type of cattle that was first cultivated in Japan and then imported to the United States in the 1970s.**

Wagyu cows have horns and are black or red in color (though most of the ones we see in the United States are black), and they're now known all over the world for their moist texture and naturally rich taste. Wagyu were originally used in agriculture—this is a strong and powerful breed, and because of their physical endurance, the cows were used mainly as draft animals to pull the plows in rice fields. Eventually, a shift in Japanese culture happened: Beef, once prohibited for consumption for religious reasons, became very popular—a famous general convinced people that eating beef made stronger soldiers. That's when the deliciousness of wagyu was discovered. Today most beef connoisseurs know wagyu for their grass-fed diet and because they have more intra-muscular fat cells than other cattle breeds. Here's the part that interests us here: Having a lot of intra-muscular fat cells means that the meat has great marbling. What that means to you is that it's got a lot of fat, and that fat is interspersed with the muscle in a way that helps create especially flavorful and tender meat. Wagyu is more expensive than other briskets, but you're paying for quality. Believe me: I don't waste money if I don't need to. But investing in wagyu has won me a lot of money, so take my word for it. I've been 100 percent open and honest with my fans—and my competitors, for that matter—that I only use wagyu beef when I compete. If you come to my cook school (which you definitely should), that's what I'll teach you to cook and that's what I'll serve you. You can get away with a cheaper type of meat if you have to—in that case, I always say that it's best to use the best product you can afford, but at least go with prime if you can, or choice if you have limited options. For something like brisket, in which the quality of the beef is more meaningful than any rub or sauce could help you approximate, my money is on using wagyu beef.

How do you trim a brisket?

A brisket is a fatty cut of meat, and you need fat for smoking because dry heat can dry out meat. So people often ask me if they need to bother trimming it. I understand the question: Why bother trimming it if you need the fat to give the brisket some flavor? Well, you do need to trim it—in fact, of all the cuts of meat that you could skip this step for, I do not recommend skipping it for a brisket. Why? Because a brisket has a thin yet dense membrane that covers it, and if you don't trim that, when it comes time to eat you're going to have a heck of a time getting through it; it can be unpleasant as hell to chew on. That said, you don't want to remove *all* the fat from your brisket. You're going for a perfect balance. So here's what you do: You want to locate the silvery white weblike coating on the brisket, then slowly use your hands to pull it away from the meat. You can also use a sharp paring knife to do this, too. I warn you: It can take damn near forever to get that membrane off. Take your time, though, because if you don't do it right, you're going to have brisket that's tough in some key places, and you do not want that.

There's one more reason to trim a brisket: You want your rub to stick to the brisket's meat and fat to flavor it and make that seared coating we pitmasters have termed "bark." If there's a membrane blocking the meat, your rub won't adhere well and it won't be able to do its job.

Remember: The goal of trimming a brisket is to set yourself up for a great cook. Try to imagine what the brisket is going to look like when it's finished smoking. For example, don't leave any point edges sticking up. They'll likely fall right off or burn. Try not to get too close to the meat when trimming, or you'll leave some bald patches without any fat. So don't trim too much, but you've got to trim enough so that the rub adheres nicely and you don't end up with a piece of meat that is tough to chew when fully cooked. If you don't like to waste anything, save what you trim off for sausage and it'll be delicious.

BRISKET TRIMMING TIPS

1. Use a sharp paring knife. A 3- to 5-inch blade is what's best for this job.

2. Start by cutting off any thick chunks of fat.

3. Hold your knife parallel to the meat while trimming. Be careful not to cut too deeply into the meat; take care to make shallow horizontal cuts. Remove a little bit at a time (do not scalp your brisket), and do it as smoothly as you can.

4. Next, remove the silver skin. You may be able to do this by pulling at it with your fingers, gripping with a kitchen towel and pulling, or you can use a thin sharp boning or paring knife.

HOW TO TRIM A BRISKET

Q:

How do you smoke brisket?

A:

This is the very best way I know how to do it, and I'm sharing it with you.
Note that I always inject my briskets with marinade. When competing, I never skip it. Injecting not only adds additional beefy flavor to the brisket but also adds some much-needed moisture into the meat. Drying out is always a risk for a big, tough cut like brisket; an injection is your best insurance against that. Don't forget to read my injecting advice before you get started (page 66).

Note that I call for hickory rub in all of these beef recipes, but it's especially crucial for brisket: This rub has very little sugar, and beef does not need any added sweetness. You should buy my rub, of course, but make sure that whatever rub you use doesn't have a lot of sugar or sweetness in it. If you are in pinch for a rub, combine salt, freshly ground pepper, and granulated garlic—that'll work for any beef dish you want to smoke.

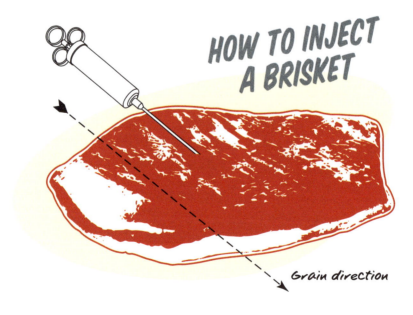

HOW TO INJECT A BRISKET

Grain direction

MYRON MIXON'S BRISKET

Make sure you have an insulated blanket ready to go.

ingredients

1 (15- to 20-pound) whole untrimmed brisket, preferably wagyu beef

¾ cup Jack's Old South Hickory Rub or make your own (page 72)

1 recipe Beef Marinade (page 68), divided for injection

tools

1 solid cutting board

1 sharp boning or paring knife

2 aluminum baking pans

1 heavy-duty meat injector

1 insulated moving blanket

Trim your brisket (page 221).

Fit the brisket snugly and fat side up in an aluminum baking pan. Make sure the pan is large enough to fit the whole brisket but not so large that the brisket slides around too much in it. Inject the brisket (see how on page 222): You want to inject half of the marinade—16 ounces total. Do that by simply eyeballing 1-inch squares and injecting the marinade all over the brisket. Once you've injected 16 ounces of liquid, flip the brisket over so that it's fat side down and pour the remaining marinade over the meat. Cover the pan tightly with aluminum foil and refrigerate at least six hours, or preferably overnight.

Thirty minutes before you are ready to smoke your brisket, prepare your smoker and heat it to 350°F. You can also use a gas grill, but you'll need to prepare it for smoking (see page 46).

Remove the brisket from the marinade, discard the marinade, and use paper towels or a clean kitchen towel to pat the brisket dry all over. Using your hands, apply the beef rub all over the meat. Place the brisket snugly in a clean aluminum baking pan. Place the pan in the smoker, close smoker cover, and smoke for 2½ hours.

Remove the pan from the smoker and cover it with aluminum foil. Put it back into the smoker and cook for another 1½ hours, or until the temperature in the point end of the brisket reaches 205°F.

recipe continues

Remove the pan from the smoker. Wrap the pan, still covered with foil, in the insulated blanket. Let it rest at room temperature in a cool dry place for no less than 3 hours; 4 hours is optimal.

After 3 to 4 hours of resting, unwrap the pan from the blanket. Discard the foil, and then transfer the brisket to a cutting board, taking care to save the accumulated pan juices. Let the brisket continue resting on the cutting board. Strain the pan juices of all grease, and then pour the juices into a medium saucepan. Warm the juices over medium heat and allow them to come to a simmer. Meanwhile, using a large serrated knife, slice the brisket against the grain into slices of about ⅛- to ¼-inch thick, depending on your taste. Try to make the slices as consistent as possible. Place the slices on a warm platter and pour the juices over them. Serve immediately.

*How do you maintain
a brisket's temperature?*

This is a great question, and I get it all the time. It's great because it acknowledges the fact that you've got to keep the temperature consistent in your smoker if you want your meat to come out tasty and delicious. It also acknowledges that when it comes to brisket, there are two points in the cooking process when the temperature is important.

MAINTAINING THE TEMPERATURE IN THE SMOKER

— Do not open your smoker if you don't have to. Every time you open it, you lower the temperature inside by 5 degrees.

— Use a water pan in your smoker (see page 51 for instructions and explanations).

— Use an external thermometer and check your smoker for fluctuations in your heat every 15 minutes and make the necessary adjustments.

MAINTAINING THE TEMPERATURE WHILE THE BRISKET RESTS

This is why you need the insulated blanket. I have explained for years that I did not invent this technique, but I sure have benefited from it. It started when I ran into a guy at a gas station in Perry, Georgia, who happened to know I was into barbecue—probably because he'd seen me towing my rig when leaving town for a competition. He said he was from Texas and asked me if I cooked brisket. I said I did. And he told me that he was going to let me in on a little secret, which was that he thought the best way to make it tender is to let it rest while it's wrapped in a blanket. This way, he said, the temperature of the meat always stays nice and consistent. So I tried it out—at first with an old sleeping bag that I still had from my childhood. It worked like a charm. Then I remembered that I had some old moving blankets somewhere, so I tried that and I've used them ever since. These insulated blankets hold the heat really well, they're strong (which is why they're used for wrapping stuff when moving), and I don't give a damn if beef juice gets on them when I cook.

How do you <u>get</u> a good smoke ring?

If you've been around someone who is seriously into barbecue for any amount of time, you've probably heard the term "smoke ring." It's something people who are into the barbecue lifestyle like to talk about, to show you that they know a thing or two about how to cook brisket or about advanced barbecue techniques. Let me demystify it for those who don't know: A smoke ring is the name for the thin pink line just below the brisket's surface that is formed under certain smoking conditions. It actually has a scientific explanation: A smoke ring is formed as a chemical reaction when nitric acid builds up on the meat's surface and is then absorbed by the meat. It's often mentioned in the same breath as brisket, but in fact, you should find smoke rings on ribs and pork, too.

There are a lot of different theories out there about how to get a good pink smoke ring on your meat, which just tells you that there are a number of halfway decent ways to go about it. For competition purposes, a smoke ring should be substantial enough to be visible in every slice, consistent in size, and long enough to go all the way around the meat. My three tips for getting a good smoke ring every time are:

1. Make sure you do a really thorough job of trimming your brisket (page 221). If you leave too much fat on it, there won't be a smoke ring. On the other hand, if you trim off too much fat, there can't be a smoke ring. So trim the fat without balding the brisket.

2. Make sure you do a good job applying rub to your brisket: Make sure that the rub has enough salt in it (my recipe does: page 72), and that you pat the rub in a consistently thick layer and apply it all over both sides of the meat.

3. Use the water-pan method (page 51) for keeping the heat and moisture level consistent in your smoker.

BRISKET SMOKE RING

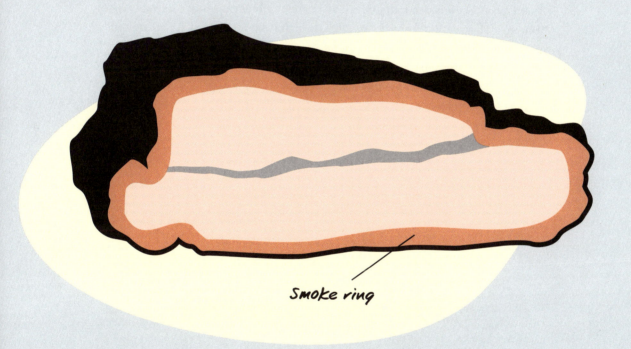

Smoke ring

Q:

How do I make burnt ends?

A:

Burnt brisket ends are a delicacy for barbecue lovers. They're not really "burnt." They're little smoky and crispy meat sponges that have soaked up delicious cooking juices. They're often cubed because they are the ends of the brisket that are too narrow to slice. Old-school barbecue competition guys like to eat them as a treat for themselves, but they are also part of the judging in competitive barbecue contests, so it's especially important to get the brisket ends consistent not only in flavor but in size. A lot folks think they're the most delicious pieces of the brisket, but that might also be because you don't get a whole lot of burnt ends out of less than a whole brisket—not to mention the fact that they require even more work than just the cooking of the brisket itself. So they're definitely treasured when they come off anyone's smoker.

There are a couple of different ways to get good burnt ends. Method One is for your casual backyard barbecue. Method Two is how to do it at a competition—or when you feel you really need to impress folks.

BACKYARD BARBECUING BURNT ENDS

Cook the brisket as described in my method (page 223). Make sure your smoker is heated to 350°F and you're maintaining that temperature. Trim off the ends of a cooked brisket that are too narrow to slice. Chop these "ends" into same-size pieces (I do cubes), put them in a clean aluminum pan, brush them with a little sauce (page 77), cover them with foil, and put them back on the smoker for an additional hour. You can serve these with the pan juice that it cooked in, or with some barbecue sauce.

CHAMPIONSHIP-WINNING BURNT ENDS

Cook the brisket as described in my method (page 223). Wrap it in a blanket and let it rest for 2 hours. After 2 hours, unwrap the brisket and use a sharp boning knife to remove the bottom section of it; what you're about to do is strategically remove the point end of the brisket. You can do this easily because there is a fatty membrane that separates the bottom of the point piece from the top, and it will break off easily by following that membrane with your knife. Simply slide your knife along the fatty membrane to cut off the point end. Then use your knife's blade to scrape away the fat from the membrane side of the bottom piece, and then season the piece all over with kosher salt and freshly ground black pepper. Place that seasoned piece directly on the smoker. Cook for 2 hours at 350°F.

Meanwhile, pour any accumulated pan drippings from the brisket into a grease separator and set aside. Place the top portion of the brisket back in the pan, wrap it in foil, and rewrap it in the blanket to continue resting.

After 2 hours, remove the burnt end portion from the smoker. Let it rest on a cutting board for at least 30 minutes. Then cut the meat into equal-size pieces, aiming for ½-inch cubes.

Place the cubes in a small pan and add the reserved strained brisket juices. Cover the pan and place in the smoker for 30 minutes. Remove and serve immediately, with or without the whole brisket slices.

"Old-school barbecue competition guys like to eat burnt ends as a treat for themselves."

How do you make a brisket sandwich as good as one from a barbecue joint?

The first thing you're going to do is follow my brisket method to the letter (page 223). Then what you're going to is this:

If you want to make sandwiches with your brisket, slice the meat on the thinner side (about ⅛ inch thick) and reserve the juices. It's best to hold the slices of brisket in these juices or to at least pour some of the juice over the slices before laying them on bread.

If you're ready to make your sandwich as soon as the brisket is ready to serve, you'll be good to go with just brisket slices and soft white bread (or a potato roll). Barbecue sauce, pickles, and coleslaw (page 297) are optional. You can make a great brisket sandwich using leftover slices of brisket. It can be served cold, or you can gently warm the meat if you prefer.

Here is a good variation if you want to get creative:

BRISKET SANDWICH WITH PEPPERS AND ONIONS

MAKES 4 SANDWICHES

ingredients

2 tablespoons olive oil

1 large sweet onion, such as Vidalia, thinly sliced

Kosher salt, to taste

Freshly ground black pepper, to taste

2 cloves garlic, chopped

1 bell pepper, thinly sliced

1 tablespoon Dijon mustard

1 tablespoon Worcestershire sauce

1 teaspoon Louisiana-style hot sauce

1 tablespoon flour

1 cup beef or chicken stock

1 cup Jack's Old South Hickory Sauce or make your own (see page 77)

4 large crusty round sandwich rolls

1½ pounds leftover brisket, cut into thin slices

Heat the olive oil in a medium skillet over medium heat. Add the onion, season with salt and pepper to taste. Cook, stirring occasionally, for 7 to 8 minutes, or until the onion has softened and begun to brown. Add the garlic, bell pepper, mustard, Worcestershire, and hot sauce to the pan. Continue to cook, stirring occasionally, until the peppers are soft and the onions are brown, about 7 minutes more.

Add the flour and cook, stirring constantly, for about 1 minute, then slowly add the stock to the pan. While stirring constantly, bring to a simmer and then continue to stir for 3 to 4 minutes, until the mixture has thickened. Remove from the heat.

Cut the rolls in half and toast to desired doneness in a toaster oven. Spread barbecue sauce on each side. Add the brisket slices to the onion-pepper mixture in the pan and stir just to combine. Once brisket is warm, transfer the brisket slices along with some onions and peppers into each sandwich. Serve immediately.

What's the easiest way to smoke brisket?

The down-and-dirty fast 'n' easy way to make a brisket is to buy a smaller one that will cook faster. This is what I do when I'm not cooking in a competition. A five-pound flat-cut brisket is just perfect for a Sunday family supper. Here's how I make it:

EASY BACKYARD BRISKET

SERVES 8

ingredients

1 (5-pound) flat-cut brisket, trimmed (see page 221 for trimming advice)

1 recipe Beef Marinade (page 68)

½ cup Jack's Old South Hickory Rub or make your own (see page 72)

2 cups Jack's Old South Hickory Sauce or make your own (see page 77)

Place the brisket in an aluminum pan. Pour the marinade over it. Cover and refrigerate for 6 hours, or preferably overnight.

Thirty minutes before you are ready to cook the brisket, heat a smoker to 350°F. Alternatively, prepare a charcoal grill for smoking.

Remove the brisket from the marinade and discard the marinade. Using paper towels or a clean kitchen towel, pat the brisket dry all over. Using your hands, apply the rub all over the meat. Place the brisket in a clean aluminum baking pan, place the plan in the smoker, and cook uncovered for 1 hour. Remove the pan from the smoker and cover it with aluminum foil. Put it back on the smoker and cook for another 30 to 45 minutes, until the internal temperature registers 205°F.

Remove the pan from the smoker and let the brisket rest, covered, for at least 30 minutes. One hour is preferable.

Remove the brisket from the pan and transfer it to a cutting board, reserving the accumulated pan juices. Using a sharp serrated knife, slice the brisket against the grain in slices about ⅛ to ¼ inch thick. Try to cut the slices in a consistent size. Place the slices on a warm platter, pour the pan juices over the brisket slices, and serve immediately.

STEAK!

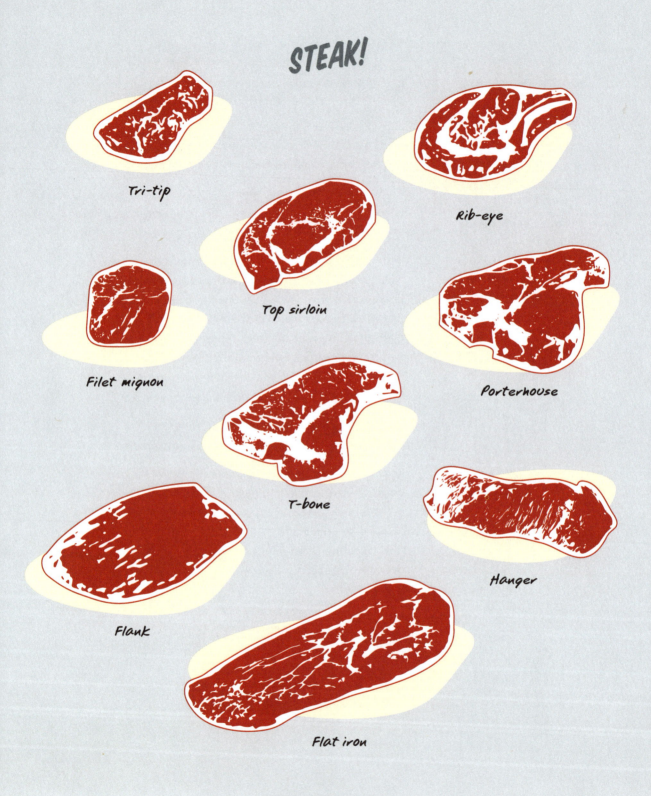

Tri-tip

Rib-eye

Top sirloin

Filet mignon

Porterhouse

T-bone

Hanger

Flank

Flat iron

Q:

What's your favorite cut of steak?

A:

I love a rib-eye. For me, it's the best steak there is. It's very tender and flavorful because it comes from the rib section. To cook a rib-eye right, you want it to be thick, and you want it to be the best beef you can afford (see my note about wagyu, page 219).

You can find many different ways to cook beef all around the world. They all involve fire, but there are all sorts of methods beyond that. Remember that the thickness of the cut is the number-one predictor of your cooking time.

Below is a list that will show you the best cooking methods for each cut. This should help you figure out what is best to smoke, grill, or roast in the oven:

Whole brisket: 18 to 20 pounds, or a smaller version (but do not smoke a brisket that is less than 5 pounds—it's too easy to dry out those small ones; braise that sucker instead)

Prime rib: a large one that's 7 ribs or so and 16 to 18 pounds, or one as small as 3 ribs that's half that weight, but don't go smaller or you'll risk drying out the meat; for a smaller rib roast, cook in the oven

Beef tenderloin: the bigger the better, ideally 4 to 5 pounds or larger; don't smoke one that's less than 2 pounds, or you'll risk drying it out

Beef ribs: see page 197 in my rib chapter for my prize-winning method in a smoker

The best cuts of meat to grill over direct heat and a hot flame:

Most cuts of steak (though some need marinating to soften, tenderize, and flavor the meat, such as flank steaks and skirt steaks) are best to grill over direct heat and a hot flame

Should I grill or smoke my steak?

People ask me variations of this question a lot, and I never know exactly how to answer: How you like your steak cooked is a matter of taste. There could be any number of factors that go into shaping that taste, including the quality of the meat that is available to you depending on the knowledge of the person who is doing the steak cooking.

I am a medium-rare guy. My dad, Jack, was all about well-done steak, though. I don't know exactly what it was, but his idea of a good steak was one that was so cooked you couldn't mistake it for something that had once been alive. There are many differences between me and my dad that go way beyond our steak preferences, but one of the things we always agreed on was the fact that we liked eating it. He liked it so much, and it was such a break from all the hog we ate, that he made sure we ate steak every Saturday night. One of the reasons I became a pitmaster was because one Saturday when I eight or nine years old, my dad said I could cook the steaks for supper. I was very nervous—my dad was a hard man who lost his temper when someone spilled iced tea at the table. All I could think about was what he would do if I messed up his steaks—I didn't know then that "well done" practically meant "impossible to screw up." Needless to say, they turned out great. And then from that point forward, I was interested in anything to do with fire, and anything to do with fire especially when it was cooking meat.

So, I can tell you how to grill a perfect steak, a rib-eye just the way I like it. Then I'm going to give you a recipe for my dad's steak of choice, a smoked T-bone. Finally, I'm going to give you a recipe for a good dinner on a busy weeknight: a flank steak you can marinate in advance, throw on the grill, and get on the table within ten minutes. When you see me at the next contest, let me know which one you like best.

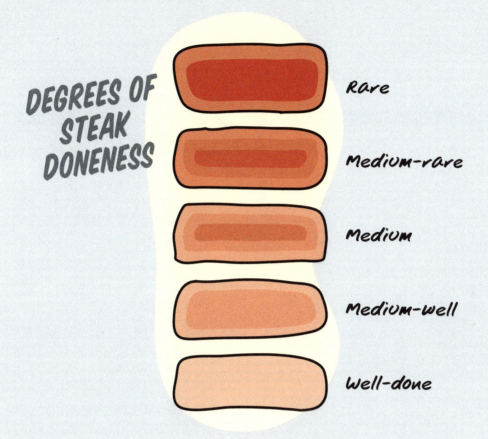

DEGREES OF STEAK DONENESS

Rare

Medium-rare

Medium

Medium-well

Well-done

TWO SECRETS TO A GREAT STEAK, NO MATTER THE CUT OR THE METHOD:

1. The quality of the meat (see page 219 for my note about wagyu beef).

2. Creating a seared crust that locks in the steak's juices and flavors until you're ready to cut into it. You get that crust by cooking the steak over dry heat, which you have in both a very hot grill and also with a smoker. So whichever method you choose for your steak—grilling or smoking—you can't lose.

GRILLED RIB-EYES WITH HOMEMADE STEAK SAUCE

A rib-eye is great for grilling because you don't have to do anything to it to make it taste good. You just need to know how to grill.

ingredients

FOR THE STEAK:

4 (16-ounce, 1½- to 1¾-inch-thick) rib-eye steaks, cut "cowboy style" (that is, with the bone in)

2 tablespoons Jack's Old South Hickory Rub or make your own (see page 72)

¼ cup extra-virgin olive oil

FOR THE SAUCE:

8 tablespoons (1 stick) unsalted butter

1 tablespoon dark brown sugar

1 teaspoon lemon juice

¼ cup tomato paste

Preheat all grates of a well-oiled charcoal or gas grill to high heat, about 400°F.

Season the steaks with rub on both sides and work it in with your hands. Using your hands or a brush, evenly—but lightly—coat the steaks with olive oil.

Place the steaks on the grate, decrease the heat to medium, close the lid, and do not move the steaks until they are well marked and have a light char. Flip them, close the lid, and continue to cook with the lid down to desired doneness, about 5 minutes per side for rare, about 6 minutes per side for medium rare, about 7 minutes per side for medium, and 9 to 10 minutes per side for medium-well to well-done.

Transfer the steaks to a platter and cover with aluminum foil. Let rest for 10 minutes.

Make your steak sauce: Collect ¼ cup of the pan drippings from the platter. Combine the juices with all of the sauce ingredients in a small saucepan. Over medium heat, whisk continuously to combine. Let the sauce just come to a boil, then remove the pan from the heat and set it aside.

To serve the steak, use a sharp knife to cut the meat across the grain in thick diagonal slices. Pour the sauce over the slices, if you like, or serve it on the side for dipping.

SMOKED T-BONE

SERVES 4 TO 6

ingredients

4 (16-ounce, 1½-inch-thick) T-bone steaks

Distilled white vinegar

Kosher salt, to taste

Freshly ground black pepper, to taste

Spritz the steaks all over with white vinegar. Then season them liberally all over with salt and pepper.

A half hour before you're ready to cook the steaks, heat the smoker to 300°F.

When you're ready to cook the steak, set it in the smoker. Close the smoker and let the steak smoke for 10 minutes. After 10 minutes, open the smoker, flip the steak, close the smoker, and smoke the steak for 10 minutes more.

To test for doneness, press the top of the steak with your index finger: Rare will be soft and yielding; medium will be firmer; well-done steak will be quite firm. You can also use an instant-read meat thermometer inserted from the side. For medium rare, cook to 130°F; for medium, cook to 140°F; anything over 155°F is well-done (note that the meat will continue to cook while it's resting and the temperature will slightly increase).

When the steak is cooked to your desired doneness, transfer it to a wooden cutting board, cover it loosely with foil, and let it rest for 10 minutes.

GRILLED FLANK STEAK

A flank steak is lean and boneless, but it's not tender: It comes from the underside of the cow, and on its own it's thin and tough. But it's awfully flavorful and worth cooking—if you season and sear it right, you can bring out its rich, beefy essence and its pleasingly chewy texture. It's good on its own with a baked potato, but it's also great to throw on top of a Caesar salad, or stuff slices into tacos and burritos. Make sure you always cut a flank steak against the grain for maximum tenderness.

ingredients

1 tablespoon Jack's Old South Hickory Rub or make your own (see page 72)

3 tablespoons dark beer

3 tablespoons Jack's Old South Hickory Sauce or make your own (see page 77)

2 teaspoons brown sugar

2 (1½-pound) flank steaks

Kosher salt, to taste

Freshly ground black pepper, to taste

In a medium nonreactive bowl, combine the rub, beer, sauce, and sugar.

Heat a charcoal or gas grill to medium-high heat, about 400°F, making sure your grate is clean and well oiled.

Arrange the steaks on a baking sheet and rub them all over with the spice and beer mixture. Let the steaks stand for 10 minutes to absorb the rub.

Season the steaks lightly with salt and pepper. Grill them uncovered, turning once, until the steaks are medium rare, about 8 minutes total cooking time. Transfer the steaks from the grill to a cutting board. Let the steaks rest for 10 minutes. Slice the meat diagonally against the grain in ¼-inch slices. Serve immediately.

Can I smoke a prime rib?

Can I smoke beef tenderloin?

These two questions I hear from my fans seem to be about smoking two different cuts of meat, but to me they're connected. In fact, the main issue is the same thing. These folks are wondering about whether they can smoke cuts of meat that aren't cheap and tough like pork butts—like for when they cook for friends and family at life's celebratory events and want to do something a little more special and expensive. Maybe it's Christmas dinner, or maybe it's a family birthday. But either way I hear these questions as "Can you dress up barbecue?" And the answer is that yes, you bet you can. Here are two great recipes for your big ol' event that will impress the hell out of your guests.

SMOKED PRIME RIB

SERVES 6 TO 8

A prime rib roast is a classic elegant way to feed a crowd. I almost always have it on my own Christmas table. Most folks are stuck in the same old rut of roasting this expensive and decadent piece of meat in the oven, but I want to expand those horizons and encourage you all that it's easy to cook a prime rib on a smoker or grill. Now, what is a prime rib? Here's what you need to know. Not all prime rib roasts are created equal. The first three ribs (1 to 3) come from closer to the loin, and thus are more tender and less fatty. The second cut (ribs 4 to 7) comes from closer to the chuck or rear end, and the ribs are more dense and fatty. Since you're about to plunk down a bunch of money for this roast, it's worth it to ask your butcher for the first cut. And as I always advise, buy the best-quality beef with the most marbling that you can afford. I'm going to give you a recipe for a small roast, but you can scale it up easily for larger one. My rule of thumb for prime rib: Allow 30 minutes of smoking time per pound of beef.

ingredients

1 (7- to 8-pound) well-marbled 3-rib standing rib roast

1 recipe Beef Marinade (page 68), divided for injection

Kosher salt, to taste

Freshly ground black pepper, to taste

1½ tablespoons onion powder

1½ tablespoons garlic powder

tools

1 injector

2 aluminum baking pans

1 insulated moving blanket

Using paper towels or a clean kitchen towel, pat the roast dry all over. Place the roast in a deep aluminum baking pan. Fill an injector with half of the marinade (16 ounces) and inject all over the roast, making injections about 1 square inch apart from each other. Pour the rest of the marinade over the roast. Cover the roast with foil and refrigerate it for at least 6 hours, or overnight for the best result.

When you are ready to cook the roast, preheat a smoker to 250°F.

Take the roast out of the pan, and use paper towels or a clean kitchen towel to pat the roast dry all over. In a small bowl combine the salt, pepper, onion powder, and garlic powder. Rub the spices all over the roast. Put the roast back in the pan and transfer the pan to the smoker. Cook the roast for 5 hours, or until the internal temperature reaches 155°F on an instant-read thermometer inserted at the center of the roast.

Take the roast out of the smoker. Transfer it to a clean aluminum baking pan and cover it with aluminum foil. Wrap the pan in an insulated moving blanket. Let it rest in a cool dry place for 1 hour.

Unwrap the pan and transfer the roast to a cutting board, reserving any pan drippings.

In a medium saucepan over medium heat, bring the reserved pan juices to a simmer. Stirring occasionally, allow the juices to simmer for about 5 minutes, until heated through but not boiling. Pour the heated drippings over the roast. Carve it, and serve immediately.

COCA-COLA SMOKED BEEF TENDERLOIN

Beef tenderloin is a showstopper. It is as delicate and as flavorful as it comes, so you have to handle it with care. But the good news is that it doesn't need a whole lot of work to make it delicious. For example, it's got so much natural flavor that it wouldn't even benefit from injecting it with a flavor-building solution. The most important rule of thumb for cooking beef tenderloin: Do not overcook it. It'll become tough and ruined. The best way to enjoy beef tenderloin is medium rare; if you like your meat well-done like my daddy did, cook another cut of meat, like the T-bone instead (page 241).

ingredients

1 (2¾- to 3-pound) beef tenderloin roast

4 cups beef broth

½ cup distilled white vinegar

1 cup packed dark brown sugar

1 (12-ounce) can Coca-Cola

Using paper towels or a clean kitchen towel, pat the tenderloin dry all over. In a large deep aluminum or other roasting pan, stir together the broth, vinegar, brown sugar, and Coca-Cola. Add the tenderloin and marinate, covered, in the refrigerator for at least 4 hours, or overnight.

When you are ready to cook the tenderloin, heat the smoker to 275°F.

Discard the marinade and transfer the tenderloin to a clean, large, deep aluminum or other roasting pan. Put the pan in the smoker and cook for about 1½ hours, or until the internal temperature at the center of the tenderloin reaches 155°F. Transfer the tenderloin to a cutting board and let it rest for 10 minutes.

Cut the tenderloin crosswise into ½-inch thick slices, and serve.

What's your idea of a great burger?

I'm pretty open about my secret to a great burger: You've got to smoke it first, then sear it. It may sound crazy, but I guarantee that you have not tasted a better burger. First you smoke the burger, then you sear it afterward to seal in the moisture with a good crust. I dreamed up this technique myself, and I was inspired to do so because I wanted to do the burger in the smoker—I love the flavor of meat that has been kissed with smoke, so I started with that idea and then built this burger-cooking technique around it.

THE SMOKED AND SEARED BURGER

If I'm going to indulge in a burger, I don't mess around: I like to make 'em with about ½ pound of ground beef apiece. And yes, if you don't feel like firing up your smoker, you can still enjoy this burger by doing the first step in the oven.

ingredients

1 pound ground beef, the best and freshest you can afford

1 (1-ounce) packet dry ranch-flavored salad-dressing mix

3 tablespoons Jack's Old South Hickory Rub or make your own (see page 72)

2 tablespoons unsalted butter

2 slices sharp cheddar cheese

2 slices smoked Canadian bacon

Two large soft white hamburger buns

OPTIONAL TOPPINGS:

Mayonnaise

Iceberg lettuce

Ripe thick tomato slices

Sliced pickles

A half hour before you're ready to cook your burger, preheat a smoker to 300°F. (If you're cooking these in the oven instead, preheat the oven to 300°F.)

In a medium nonreactive bowl, combine the ground beef with the ranch dressing mix and the rub. Using your hands, mix gently to combine, taking care not to overwork the meat. Form into two patties of equal size (or three or four patties, if you like smaller burgers).

Transfer the burgers to a small and shallow aluminum baking pan. Refrigerate them until the smoker (or oven) is ready. Then place the pan in the smoker (or oven). For medium-rare burgers, smoke for 15 minutes, or for medium-well burgers, go to 30 minutes.

Remove the burger pan from the smoker (or oven) and allow the burgers to rest, uncovered, while you melt the butter in a medium skillet over medium heat on a stovetop or gas grill (the smoker won't be hot enough to give you a good sear). When the butter is melted but not smoking, use a spatula to slide the burgers carefully into the skillet. Cook for about 3 minutes, just until they're seared on one side and a nice crust has formed, then flip them and do the same on the other side. Top them with cheddar and then slide the burgers onto a platter and let them rest, lightly covered with aluminum foil.

While the burgers rest, wipe out the pan. Over medium heat in that same pan, cook the Canadian bacon about 2 minutes

recipe continues

per side, until each side is lightly crispy. Using a spatula, slide the Canadian bacon onto paper towels to absorb any excess grease.

Toast the buns in your smoker or on a low setting in the toaster oven. Smear a little mayonnaise on the bottom half of each bun. Top with the cheeseburgers, a slice of Canadian bacon, a nice piece of cold, crisp Iceberg lettuce, a slice of ripe tomato, and pickles. Smear the inside top of each bun with a little more mayonnaise. That's barbecue burger heaven right there.

Besides great BBQ, we have a hell of a burger at my restaurant in Alexandria, Virginia. (See page 253 for our brunch burger.)

Q:

What if I just want to grill a burger? What's the best way?

A:

Simply grilling a burger is quick and easy, and everyone who has a backyard or a fire escape or a tailgating situation should learn how to do it well. Grilling your burgers doesn't give them that smoke-kissed flavor I love (see page 249), but they'll still be damn good. Here's how to grill a great burger:

MYRON MIXON'S GRILLED CHEESEBURGERS

SERVES 2

ingredients

1 pound ground beef, the best and freshest you can afford

1 (1-ounce) packet dry ranch-flavored salad-dressing mix

3 tablespoons Jack's Old South Hickory Rub or make your own (see page 72)

2 slices sharp cheddar cheese

Two large soft white hamburger buns

Prepare a medium-hot fire in your grill. You're aiming to grill the burgers at about 425°F.

In a medium nonreactive bowl, combine the ground beef with the ranch dressing mix and the rub. Using your hands mix gently to combine, taking care not to overwork the meat. Form into two patties of equal size (or three or four patties, if you like smaller burgers).

Place the burgers on the rack directly over the coals. Cover the grill and cook the burgers to your doneness of choice: For medium-rare, I like about 6 minutes per side.

Top each burger with a slice of cheddar cheese. Transfer them to a platter and let them rest, lightly tented with aluminum foil, for 10 minutes.

Meanwhile, lightly toast the buns and butter them, if you like. Serve the cheeseburgers immediately, with your garnishes of choice.

BURGER GRILLING TIP

The more a burger is handled the more likely it is to turn out dry. So don't use forks to flip your burgers or transfer them onto the grill. You want all the juice in that burger to stay in that burger. Use a spatula, but don't flip that burger constantly, either. And don't press down on it, or poke it, or agitate that sucker in any way other than necessary.

BRUNCH BURGERS WITH PORK BELLY

All right, folks, I'm going to give you a bonus burger. This is on the menu at my restaurant Myron Mixon's Pitmaster Barbecue outside of Washington, DC, in Alexandria, Virginia, where we offer guests a big ol' Southern brunch every Sunday morning. I wanted it to be a good time for everyone, and it is. One way I insured that is by coming up with my brunch burger, which is topped with smoky pork belly instead of traditional bacon, and some good sharp cheddar. It'll cure your hangover, but you might have to spend the rest of your week at the gym.

ingredients

FOR THE PORK BELLY:

2 whole garlic cloves

1 teaspoon red pepper flakes

2 tablespoons soy sauce

2 tablespoons honey

2 tablespoons ketchup

1 8-ounce piece of pork belly

FOR THE BURGERS:

24 ounces ground beef, preferably ground chuck with 20% fat

2 teaspoons Dijon mustard

1 teaspoon Jack's Old South Original Rub or make your own (see page 72)

Kosher salt, to taste

Freshly ground black pepper, to taste

ingredients continue

Marinate the pork belly:

Combine the garlic, chili flakes, soy sauce, honey, and ketchup in a food processor to combine. Transfer into a plastic zip-top bag with the pork belly and marinate in the refrigerator for at least 2 hours, or preferably overnight.

When you are ready to cook the burgers:

Remove the pork belly from the marinade and discard the marinade. Wash the pork belly and pat it dry thoroughly. Slice the pork belly into slices of roughly ¼" thick. You should have about 12 slices. Set aside.

Heat a charcoal grill or gas grill to medium-high heat.

Line a large dinner plate with plastic wrap. In a medium-size bowl, combine the ground beef with the mustard and rub, gently kneading and taking care not to overhandle the meat, into 4 patties of equal size and thickness. Season the burgers generously with salt and pepper and transfer them to the prepared plate. Set aside.

Brush both sides of the burger buns with the melted butter and set aside.

recipe continues

4 burger buns, split

2 tablespoons unsalted butter, melted

3 tablespoons Jack's Old South Hickory Sauce or make your own (see page 77)

4 slices sharp cheddar cheese

Lettuce and tomato, for garnish

Grill the burgers directly on the grill for about 7 to 8 minutes, turning once, for medium-rare. Move the burgers away from the heat to rest on a warm (but definitely not hot) part of the grill. Top each burger with a slice of sharp cheddar cheese. Grill the cut side of the buns for about 1 minute, until toasted.

Use tongs to transfer the pork belly slices onto a hot grill and cook for about 2 minutes. Flip and repeat until the slices are to your liking; I like them crispy. Transfer the buns onto a paper towel–lined plate when cooked to desired doneness.

Brush the tops and bottoms of the buns with the barbecue sauce.

Slide the cheeseburgers onto the buns and top each one with lettuce, tomatoes, and three slices of the reserved pork belly. Serve the burgers immediately.

Can you smoke meatloaf?

I promised y'all that I'd answer all of your frequently asked questions. I also promised that in every chapter I'd take one of my favorite "oddball" questions, a unique one that I've heard while I've been teaching or doing a demo or on my social media. Here is that question. I won't lie to you: I'm choosing this "oddball" because I'm a guy who loves meatloaf. And I love meat that has been kissed by smoke. So you're damn right you can smoke meatloaf, and here's how I do it:

SMOKED MEATLOAF

MAKES 1 (9-INCH) MEATLOAF; SERVES 6

ingredients

½ cup milk (preferably whole milk, but not skim)

1 cup Jack's Old South Hickory Sauce or make your own (see page 77)

1 cup finely crushed Ritz crackers (about 20 crackers)

1½ pounds ground beef

½ pound ground pork

2 large eggs, lightly beaten

½ teaspoon ground nutmeg

½ cup grated Parmesan cheese

1 large egg, lightly beaten

1 tablespoon Jack's Old South Hickory Rub or make your own (see page 72)

Kosher salt, to taste

Freshly ground black pepper, to taste

Thirty minutes before you're ready to cook the meatloaf, prepare a smoker and heat it to 200°F. Grease a 9 by 5-inch loaf pan with cooking spray or butter.

In a large bowl, whisk together the milk and ¾ cup of the sauce. Stir in the crackers, ground beef, ground pork, eggs, nutmeg, Parmesan, beaten egg, and rub, and mix gently to combine, taking care not to overmix the meatloaf. Season to taste with salt and pepper. Pack the meat mixture into the prepared pan.

When the smoker is ready, place the meatloaf pan inside. Cover and smoke the meatloaf, checking the temperature frequently to maintain a consistent 200°F, until the internal temperature of the meatloaf registers 140°F on an instant-read thermometer, about 2 hours. At that point, brush the remaining ¼ cup of sauce on top of the meatloaf. Close the smoker and continue to smoke the meatloaf until it reaches its final temperature of 155°F, about 1 hour more. The total cooking time should be about 3 hours. Transfer the meatloaf pan to a cutting board, cover it loosely with aluminum foil, and allow it to rest for 20 minutes before slicing and serving.

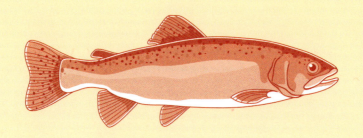

CHAPTER EIGHT

SWIMMING LESSONS

ALL ABOUT COOKING SEAFOOD & FISH

Simply Grilled
Jumbo Shrimp
page 277

Easy Smoked Salmon
page 268

Catfish
page 269

Whole Smoked Trout
page 281

Do you ever smoke fish?

Fact number one: I don't only eat barbecue. Fact number two: I'm trying to be a healthy individual, which means that like the rest of you, I'm trying to eat more fish. Fact number three: My daddy Jack's passion in life was fishing. That man loved nothing more than catching fish and bringing them home for dinner. We ate fish at least once a week, usually as a Saturday-night fish fry. My dad dragged me along so many times that going fishing began to feel like my job—I don't much enjoy it for that reason. But I do enjoy cooking fish, and I do a fish fry most Friday nights at my barbecue cooking skills class at my compound in Unadilla, Georgia.

I like smoking, grilling, and frying fish. And yes, it is a good idea for you learn how to do it, too.

HOT SMOKING FISH: THE BASICS

There are generally two ways to smoke fish. The cold-smoking technique relies on super-cold temperatures—we're talking below 160°F—and requires special equipment. It's a great technique, but I'm not the guy to teach it to you. I'm the guy to teach you about hot smoking, a process in which we're going to season the fish with spices or rubs and then smoke it in our smoker over indirect heat at about 250°F. What we're looking for here is fish that is moist and tender, perfectly cooked through, and gently kissed with the flavor of smoke.

CHOOSING YOUR FISH: BEYOND TUNA AND SALMON

Knowing which kind of fish can stand up to the rough 'n' rustic cooking technique of smoking is very important. That said, I disagree with the conventional wisdom that delicate, flaky fish can't handle the smoker. It's just a matter of technique, and I'll teach you how to do it right. Trust me on this: I have experimented with smoking just about every type of fish you can think of, and I've come to the following conclusion: Smoking is one of the tastiest and healthiest ways to cook fish. There's no oil or batter involved, and there's tons of great flavor.

PREP YOUR FISH FOR SMOKING

Know that smoked fish does not have grill marks on it. Remember: You're not cooking the fish on a very hot grate like when you grill it. You're smoking it over low heat, so it will have a slightly glossy appearance from the smoke. I do the same fish prep for all of the fish I smoke: Rub fish fillets all over with apple cider vinegar. Pat them dry thoroughly with clean paper towels or a clean kitchen towel. Then brush the fish with a little olive oil and season all over with salt and pepper or with barbecue rub (page 72), as you like.

THE FOUR STEPS TO GREAT SMOKED FISH

I favor using disposable aluminum pans for many reasons, not the least of which because they are available in all grocery stores and leave the least amount of mess for you to clean up when you're done cooking. Know that they especially come in handy when you're smoking fish. Just be sure to oil the pans before you put the fish in and put them in the smoker—that way, the fish won't stick.

Step One: Start with the freshest fish possible. Beginners should start out learning to smoke fish with firm-fleshed fish steaks like salmon, tuna, and sword-fish, whole fish like trout, char, or catfish, or firm-fleshed fillets of any of those mentioned are great. Shellfish like shrimp, oysters, and scallops are great candidates for smoking, too. With whole fish, look for clear eyes and shiny skin (not gray or dull), and when you smell it, the aroma should be salty like the sea and not have any hint of bleach or ammonia. Touch the fish with your index finger: Make sure the flesh "bounces back" and doesn't stay indented and doesn't shred.

Step Two: Make sure your grill and smoker grates are clean and well oiled. This makes cooking everything easier, but especially fish. It's a good time to clean your smoker or grill before you get out there and start cooking.

Step Three: Use the same kind of local wood in your smoker that you use to smoke your meats (see page 50). So for example, if you're in the Northwest, think about your local alder wood. If you're in the Northeast, think about your local maple wood. For me, here in Georgia, that means peach wood, and I like the way it and other fruitwoods (like cherry and apple) impart a little sweetness into the fish.

Step Four: The most crucial thing to learn when smoking fish is when it's done. Smoking food too long gives it a bitter flavor, which is especially noticeable with something delicate like fish. I'll give you times, but I want you to use visual cues. Use your eyes and your fingertips, folks: When the color of the fish turns opaque and the flesh just begins to flake when you poke it with a fork, the smoked fish is ready to come off the smoker. For shellfish, look for it to turn opaque in color and firm to the touch.

What's your favorite way to smoke fish?

People always want to know my "favorite." I'm a professional cook who wins money for his recipes and techniques. All my dishes are my favorite. I love every single one of them, and that's why I cook them; that's why I win contests with them. So let me tell you the question you really want to ask me about smoked fish: How do I cook it so that the fish comes out delicious? Let me tell you three of my favorite formulas for smoking fish here and now: for smoked fish steaks, whole fish, and fillets. Pick the one you like best and then *you* can tell *me* about your favorite.

SMOKED AND GLAZED SALMON STEAKS

SERVES 6

ingredients

FOR THE FISH:

6 (4- to-6-ounce, 1½- to preferably 2-inch-thick) salmon steaks

¼ cup apple cider vinegar

¼ cup olive oil

1 tablespoon kosher salt

1 tablespoon freshly ground black pepper

½ cup Jack's Old South Original Rub or make your own (see page 72)

FOR THE GLAZE:

2 cups Jack's Old South Vinegar sauce or make your own (see page 78)

4 ounces apricot preserves

½ cup chopped sweet onion, such as Vidalia

Prepare your smoker and heat it to 250°F.

Rub the salmon steaks all over with the vinegar, then pat the steaks dry thoroughly with paper towels or a clean kitchen towel. Brush both sides of the steaks with the olive oil, then season with the salt, pepper, and rub. Transfer the steaks into an aluminum baking pan. Place the pan in the smoker, cover, and smoke until the steaks are firm to the touch and flake when touched with a fork, 45 to 60 minutes.

While the fish is cooking, make the glaze: Combine the barbecue sauce, apricot preserves, and chopped onion in a blender. Puree to combine thoroughly, about 3 minutes. Pour the mixture into a medium saucepan. Over medium heat, bring the glaze almost to a boil, removing it from the heat just as small bubbles begin to appear at the surface. Set the glaze aside to cool.

When the fish is done, remove the pan from the smoker and use a kitchen brush to glaze the salmon steaks with the sauce. Serve warm or at room temperature.

Note: You can easily make these salmon steaks without applying the glaze; just skip that step entirely and serve the salmon steaks with some barbecue sauce on the side for dipping if you like. You can also substitute tuna, swordfish, or halibut steaks for the salmon and this recipe will work just as well. Finally, I like the way that the sweetness of the apricot preserves pairs with the barbecue sauce, but you are welcome to try other favorite flavors of preserves in its place if you prefer.

EASY SMOKED SALMON

SERVES 6 TO 8

This is one of the easiest methods of cooking fish for a little backyard dinner party with family or friends—it's simple, delicious, and smoked, my three favorite attributes for food.

ingredients

2 pounds salmon fillets, skin on

¼ cup apple cider vinegar

½ cup olive oil

¼ cup Jack's Old South Original Rub or make your own (see page 72)

1 tablespoon kosher salt

1 tablespoon freshly ground black pepper

Prepare your smoker and heat it to 250°F.

Rub the salmon fillets all over with the vinegar, then pat dry thoroughly with paper towels or a clean kitchen towel. Brush them all over with the oil, then season with the rub, salt, and pepper. Transfer the fish to an aluminum baking pan.

Place the pan in the smoker, cover, and cook until the salmon flakes easily, about 2 hours. Serve with Classic Creamy Coleslaw (page 297) if you like.

Variation 1: You can substitute 2 pounds of other fish fillets and use this same method. For example, where I live we love mullet, a fish found in coastal and tropical waters all over the world, but especially beloved down here in South Georgia and parts of Florida. It's a bony and oily fish that takes very well to smoking. You can also substitute trout fillets, pike fillets, roughy fillets, or other kinds of fish you like and use this method.

Variation 2: You can substitute the ½ cup of olive oil I call for here with ½ cup of cubed unsalted butter. Just cover the fish with the butter cubes and put it in the smoker.

SMOKED WHOLE CATFISH

To make this recipe, you're going to need to either ask a fishmonger to clean your catfish for you—the path of least resistance—or else figure out how to do it yourself. The leathery skin of catfish makes the process a little more complicated than it is for other fish. Some fishermen where I live hang the catfish from trees before they strip them, or else nail the fish heads to boards. Those techniques work great, but page 270 has another way for novices:

ingredients

1 (4- to 6-pound) catfish, cleaned

¼ cup apple cider vinegar

1 cup vegetable oil

2 tablespoons kosher salt

Freshly ground black pepper, to taste

¼ cup Jack's Old South Original Rub or make your own (see page 72)

2 cups apple juice

Prepare your smoker and heat it to 250°F.

Rub the catfish all over with the vinegar, then pat dry thoroughly with paper towels or a clean kitchen towel. Brush both sides with the oil, then season with the salt, pepper, and rub. Transfer the fish to an aluminum baking pan.

Place the pan in the smoker, cover, and smoke for 2 hours. Spritz the fish every 30 minutes with the apple juice. After two hours, gently and carefully flip the catfish. Continue smoking for 2 more hours, spritzing with the apple juice every 30 minutes, until the fish begins to flake easily. Total cooking time should be 3½ to 4 hours.

HOW TO CLEAN A CATFISH

Step One: Use a sharp fillet knife to cut behind the fish's head. Make sure to slice only through the skin and not the meat and bone beneath.

Step Two: Use your sharp knife to cut the fins off the catfish's body; if you don't, the dorsal (back) and ventral (stomach) can get in your way, so it is best to remove them. The catfish fins can be very sharp, so be careful. Side cutters work well for this because the spines can be difficult to cut through. Toss those.

Step Three: Remove the skin: Peel back some of the skin from behind the fish's neck near the gills. Grip that skin very firmly with pliers. Grip the catfish's head in one hand and the pliers holding the skin in the other hand. Gently but firmly pull back the pliers to peel off the skin, pulling forcefully toward the tail. Toss the skin.

Step Four: Remove the head and guts. Go back to the line you cut around the head and use your sharp knife to cut down and remove the head. You may need to use your hands to twist it off as a final step. If the vertebrae are very thick, you can bend the head back until the vertebrae separates to get your knife between them and cut the connective tissues so you can remove the head. To remove the guts, cut a shallow slit along the belly of the fish from where the head was all the way to the tail. Once the stomach cavity is open, you can remove all the organs and put them aside with the head. Try not to puncture anything and you will have less of a cleanup. Give the fish a rinse to make sure all organs and secretions are gone. You're ready to go. Y'all make sure you scrub your wooden cutting boards with soap and water after cleaning catfish.

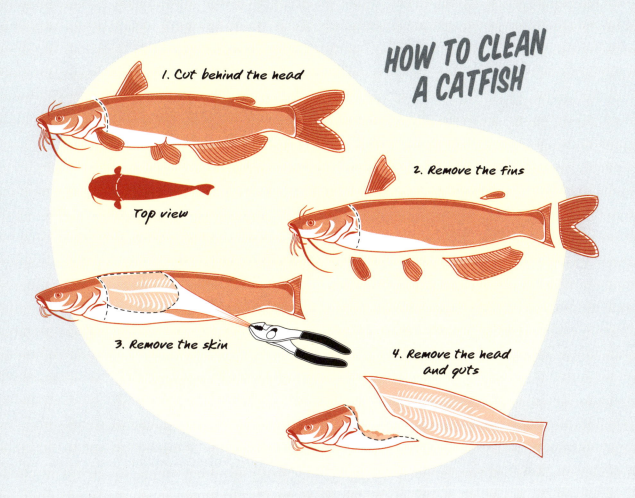

HOW TO CLEAN A CATFISH

1. Cut behind the head

Top view

2. Remove the fins

3. Remove the skin

4. Remove the head and guts

GOT FISH HEADS AND GUTS?

1. Use them as fertilizer for your garden or plants.

2. If you live near a coast, you can go crabbing: The head is great bait for crab traps.

3. Make fish stock. Just be sure that the fish head is clean. You can also freeze the head and guts until you are ready to make stock.

Can I smoke a lobster?

Just because the South is known as a poor part of the country doesn't mean we don't eat well. This whole book—in fact, my whole career—is a testament to just how well we eat. Yeah, we can smoke some lobster tails. There's nothing more delicious than these suckers, if you ask me. Makes you feel like a king to eat them in your own backyard, too.

SMOKED LOBSTER TAILS WITH FRESH CELERY SLAW

ingredients

FOR THE LOBSTER:

4 (8- to 10-ounce) lobster tails, removed from their shells

3 tablespoons olive oil

Kosher salt, to taste

Freshly ground black pepper, to taste

FOR THE CELERY SLAW:

2 tablespoons mayonnaise or sour cream

Juice of 1 lemon

3 large celery stalks, coarsely chopped

¼ head iceberg lettuce, shredded

1 tablespoon Jack's Old South Original Rub or make your own (see page 72)

FOR SERVING:

4 tablespoons (½ stick) unsalted butter, melted

Prepare your smoker and heat it to 325°F.

Prepare the lobster tails: Use kitchen shears to make shallow cuts right down the middle of the tough tail shells. Next, use your fingers to gently loosen the meat from the shell, making sure to just loosen it and not remove it entirely—you want to keep the tail meat attached at the base of the tail. Lift the meat so it is resting on top of the split shell (again, keeping it attached at the base of the tail). Use a sharp paring knife to make a shallow slit down the middle of the meat so that you can butterfly the tails and open them up like a book. Drizzle the tail meat with the olive oil and season with salt and pepper. Place the butterflied lobster tails in an aluminum baking pan.

Place the pan in the smoker, cover, and smoke for about 25 to 30 minutes, or until the lobster meat turns completely bright white and opaque and the tails begin to curl.

Meanwhile, prepare the salad: In a medium bowl, stir together the mayonnaise, lemon juice, celery, lettuce, and rub. Set aside.

Timing is key here: When you're ready to remove the lobster from the smoker, you don't want to let it cool completely, or the meat will begin to toughen up. So remove the lobster from the smoker, transfer to serving plates immediately, and for a dramatic presentation serve the tails in their shells next to the salad, drizzling the butter over the tail meat. Alternatively, you can remove the tails from their shells and serve them directly on top of the salad with the melted butter drizzled over the top of the tails.

What's the best way to smoke/grill/barbecue shrimp?

If you've gotten to this point in the book, you now know that you can smoke just about any protein there is and make it taste good. Hot smoking shrimp is a pretty quick and easy thing to do, and the smoky flavor from this cooking process really brings out the natural sweetness of the shrimp. And I love that.

There are a couple of things you need to know about smoking shrimp: You can do it with the shells on or off, but I like it better with the shells on—it ensures moister shrimp that won't dry out easily. Larger shrimp hold up better to the smoking process than smaller ones do. Finally, we're going to do what I call a "quick brine" on the shrimp before we smoke them, so leave yourself a couple hours in advance of when you want to eat these suckers to properly prepare them. You'll also need to refrigerate them to cool and firm up before you serve them, so allow thirty minutes for that as well.

Note: Smoking shrimp is a great thing to do *when you're already using your smoker to smoke other things.* It doesn't take much extra effort to throw the shrimp in the smoker if you're already using it anyway, and then you can have these smoked shrimp around for appetizers. That's a smart way to entertain, right there.

Finally, about grilling shrimp: This is not a grilling cookbook. I am a damn good griller, which shouldn't be hard for anyone to believe considering how much time I spend cooking outside. But I am a world champion barbecue pitmaster, and that means my specialty is smoking and cooking at lower temperatures. Still, occasionally in these pages I've given you advice and formulas for how to grill certain favorite dishes of mine. Since grilling shrimp is fast and easy, I'm going to give you a great technique for how to do it the way I do it.

HOW TO PEEL AND DEVEIN SHRIMP

You want to remove the thin black string–looking thing that runs along the back of the shrimp just beneath the shell's surface not only because it's unattractive but also because it adds real grittiness to the shrimp. The black "string" is the shrimp's digestive tract, and although it's not harmful if you accidentally ingest one, you should remove it before cooking. Most of the time it's fairly easy to spot—sometimes it's even prominent—but occasionally it's more clear than dark and requires some poking around. Either way, this is an easy thing to do. It's also best and most easily done by hand. To peel raw shrimp, start underneath, where their legs are attached. Pull the legs off and discard. Use your thumbs to crack the shell open along the underside (where the shell is softer) and pull off the shell—you can save the shells to make shrimp stock or discard them. If you like you can leave the last tail segment, which both looks nice for serving and also gives a nice handle for holding onto while you're eating. Devein the shrimp using a sharp paring knife to make a shallow slit down the middle of the back to expose the black intestine. Pull out the black string of intestine and discard.

HOW TO DEVEIN A SHRIMP

1. Remove legs

2. Remove shell

3. Make a shallow cut

4. Pull out the "vein"

SMOKED SHRIMP

2½ to 3 pounds fresh large shrimp, peeled or unpeeled (21 to 25 count per pound)

¼ cup kosher salt

Prepare the shrimp: Put the shrimp in a shallow pan. Sprinkle with the salt and rub it all over each shrimp. Cover with plastic wrap and transfer to the fridge to rest for 2 hours.

Prepare the smoker and heat it to 225°F.

When you are ready to cook the shrimp, remove them from the refrigerator and carefully rinse the salt from each shrimp under cold water; use paper towels or a clean kitchen towel to dry them well. Transfer the shrimp to an aluminum baking pan. Transfer the pan to the smoker, cover, and smoke the shrimp for 15 to 30 minutes, until their shells turn coral or, if unpeeled, the shrimp is totally white and opaque.

Remove the pan from the smoker and let the shrimp rest uncovered in the fridge for at least 30 minutes before serving.

SIMPLY GRILLED JUMBO SHRIMP

SERVES 4

You don't need a special grill basket or rack to grill shrimp, but it is easier if you grill them on skewers, so that's what I'm recommending here. If you have wooden skewers, make sure you've soaked them in water at least one hour and preferably 3. If you love this recipe you might want to invest in some good metal ones.

ingredients

2 pounds jumbo shrimp, in their shells

2 tablespoons olive oil

2 tablespoons fresh lemon juice

Kosher salt, to taste

Freshly ground black pepper, to taste

Cut each shrimp in half lengthwise, starting at the underside and making a shallow cut (don't cut all the way through) to the top shell. Unfold the shrimp (open them like a book) and devein them, then rinse them under cold running water. Pat the shrimp dry with paper towels or a clean kitchen towel. Transfer the shrimp to an aluminum baking pan, drizzle them with the olive oil and lemon juice, and season them with salt and pepper. Cover with plastic wrap and marinate in the refrigerator for 30 minutes, flipping them over at the 15-minute mark.

Preheat your grill to high heat.

When you're ready to cook, remove the shrimp from the refrigerator and thread them onto skewers. Because these are jumbo, you may need to use 2 skewers per shrimp: To do that, lay each shrimp flat and pin open crosswise with 2 skewers, one each, top and bottom.

Arrange the shrimp cut side down on the grill, turning with tongs, until browned on the outside and firm and pink inside, about 2 minutes per side.

Remove the skewers from the grill, transfer the shrimp onto plates or a platter, and serve immediately.

BARBECUE SHRIMP

2 pounds large fresh or defrosted shrimp (21 to 25 count per pound)

1 cup olive oil

1 teaspoon kosher salt

1 teaspoon freshly ground black pepper

1 tablespoon Jack's Old South Original Rub or make your own (see page 72)

¾ cup Jack's Old South Hickory Sauce or make your own (see page 77)

Fresh lemons, quartered, for serving (optional)

Cut each shrimp in half lengthwise, starting at the underside and making a shallow cut (don't cut all the way through) to the top shell. Unfold the shrimp (open them like a book) and devein them, then rinse them under cold running water. Pat the shrimp dry with paper towels or a clean kitchen towel. Thread the shrimp onto skewers. Place the skewers in a row in an aluminum baking pan. Brush the shrimp with the olive oil using a basting brush. Then season the shrimp with the salt, pepper, and rub, all over and on both sides. Pour the sauce over the shrimp skewers, turning them over, until all the shrimp are coated. Cover with plastic wrap and let the shrimp marinate in the refrigerator for 30 minutes.

When you're ready to cook, prepare a medium-hot fire in your grill.

Remove the shrimp skewers from the sauce marinade. Reserve the marinade and transfer it to a small saucepan. Bring the marinade to a boil over medium-high heat, let simmer for 2 minutes, then set aside. Transfer the shrimp skewers directly over the coals and cook until the shrimp are pink on both sides, 2 to 3 minutes per side, taking care not to overcook. Baste with the reserved warm sauce while cooking. Serve immediately with fresh lemons on the side, if you like.

SMOKED PRAWNS

SERVES 4 TO 6

Here's a little delicacy for you to try out at home. A lot of folks think that prawns are just big shrimp, but even though they look like it, that's not really true. Their bodies are a little different—prawns are long and straight and not curved like shrimp, and they only live in fresh water (while shrimp live in salt water). The difference doesn't matter too much when it comes to cooking: You want to be sure not to overcook either one. I go for prawns when I get the chance because they're a little meatier and a little sweeter than shrimp—more like miniature lobster tails, if you ask me, and because of their size and sweetness, they take really well to smoking. This is a killer way to enjoy them.

ingredients

24 prawns or jumbo shrimp, peeled and deveined, tails left on

½ cup Jack's Old South Original Rub or make your own (see page 72)

½ cup fresh lemon juice

½ cup Jack's Old South Hickory Sauce or make your own (see page 77)

2 tablespoons honey

4 tablespoons (½ stick) unsalted butter

Prepare your smoker and heat it to 350°F.

Apply the rub to the cleaned and deveined prawns, making sure to coat them well. Thread the prawns on skewers inserted lengthwise so that the prawns stay straight and vertical. Place the skewers in a large aluminum plan, put it in the smoker, cover, and cook for 10 minutes.

While the prawns are cooking: In a medium saucepan combine the lemon juice, barbecue sauce, honey, and butter. Over medium heat, bring the sauce almost to a boil, stirring constantly, and then take the pan off the heat.

After 10 minutes, remove the prawns from the smoker, brush them all over with the sauce, and serve.

Q:

Can I smoke trout?

A:

I love smoked trout, and I think it's great that you can get it pretty much year-round at groceries and fish markets—because it's so commonly farmed these days. This is a delicious and simple dinner, and you can serve the trout with some horseradish sauce on the side—I'll give you a good, easy recipe for that, too.

Pro tip: This is excellent eating, but it requires some prep. You need to brine the fish and then let it rest in the refrigerator overnight, so be sure to give yourself a day in advance to prep the fish. Totally worth it, I promise you.

WHOLE SMOKED TROUT

SERVES 6 TO 8

ingredients

6 to 8 rainbow trout, cleaned and skin-on with pin bones removed (you can clean it yourself and I'll give you directions for how to do that—also see page 282—or you can go to your fishmonger and buy about 4 pounds of fillets that are already cleaned and boned—just make sure they still have their skins on)

1 gallon water

½ cup brown sugar

¼ cup kosher salt

Prepare the fish: Using a sharp boning knife, insert the tip of the knife into the fish's vent and make a shallow slice up to the gills. Remove the knife and reinsert it through the skin under the lower jaw, horizontally, and make a shallow horizontal slice up to the mouth. Insert your finger into the fish's throat through this chin cut. Grasping the gills from the inside, pull the chin down, firmly, toward the tail. If you do this right, the fish's guts, gills, and pec fins will come free in one clean pull. Discard those innards. Scrape away the dark bloodline that remains with a sharp knife or your thumb. Give the fish a good rinse, and it's ready to cook.

Brine the fish: Combine the water, brown sugar, and salt in a large stockpot. Bring just to the point of boiling, stirring to dissolve the salt and sugar. Let the brine cool completely.

In a clean small cooler or large zip-top bags, submerge the fish for about 3 hours.

When you're ready to cook, heat the smoker to 225°F.

Remove the fish from the brine, rinse under cold water, and pat them dry. Place the trout skin side down on a rack set in a baking pan. Cover with plastic wrap. Place the pan in the refrigerator and let rest, covered, in the refrigerator overnight. You are looking for the fish's skin to become shiny in color and sticky to the touch.

When you are ready to cook the trout, prepare your smoker and heat it to 225°F. Transfer your trout fillets to an aluminum baking pan, skin side down, separating them by at least ¼ inch. Don't overcrowd your pan; use more pans if you need to. Place the pan(s) in the smoker and cook for 1½ to 2 hours, or until the fish turns opaque and starts to flake.

HOW TO CLEAN A TROUT

1. Slice along belly from vent to gills

2. Cut under jaw to separate gills and head

3. Grasp gills and pull down, removing gills and entrails

4. Scrape away bloodline

HORSERADISH SAUCE FOR SMOKED TROUT

MAKES ABOUT 1 CUP DIP, ENOUGH FOR 6 TO 8 SERVINGS WITH FISH

You can serve the smoked trout hot or at room temperature; it's delicious either way. I like it with this horseradish sauce on the side. You can make the sauce a day in advance.

ingredients

⅔ cup heavy cream

2 tablespoons chopped fresh dill

2 tablespoons vodka, plain or lemon-flavored (optional)

4 tablespoons freshly grated or prepared horseradish (if using bottled, drain it well)

Kosher salt, to taste

Freshly ground black pepper, to taste

4 sprigs fresh dill, for garnish (optional)

In a medium bowl using a whisk, whip the cream until stiff peaks form. Fold in the chopped dill, vodka, and horseradish. Season the sauce with salt and pepper to taste. Cover and refrigerate until ready to serve. Garnish with the dill sprigs, if you like.

Do you like shrimp 'n' grits?

What kind of Southern person doesn't like shrimp 'n' grits? This dish is a classic creation of our coastal shores. Even though shrimp 'n' grits shows up in hipster restaurants in places like Brooklyn, it started out as poor-people food. Nowadays you can find shrimp 'n' grits gussied up with sautéed mushrooms and green peppers and white wine. That is good eating, but I'm going to give you an easier option.

A NOTE ABOUT GRITS

As Southern cooks know, all grits are not created equal. You've got a wide range of varieties, but they break down into three camps of ground corn. *Stone-ground grits* are made from whole dried corn kernels that have been coarsely ground between two stones of a gristmill. Because the entire kernel is ground, including the germ, stone-ground grits have a speckled appearance, a chewy texture, and a deep corn flavor. Stone-ground grits are less processed, which makes them more perishable, so store them in the freezer, not the pantry. They also take longer to cook than *quick-cooking grits* and *regular grits*. The only difference between these two types is in granulation. Quick grits are ground fine and usually cook in about 5 minutes; regular grits are a medium grind and cook in about 10 minutes. This is a classic shrimp 'n' grits recipe, and I'm calling for the old-school stone-ground type, but if you're short on time you can substitute regular grits, which should be simmered for 10 minutes instead of 30 to 40. On a busy weeknight, you might not know the difference. Sunday brunch? Go stone-ground.

SHRIMP 'N' GRITS

ingredients

2 cups water

2 cups Smoked Stock (page 93) or good-quality store-bought stock

¾ cup whole cream or half-and-half (do not use skim milk)

1 cup stone-ground grits

1 cup shredded sharp cheddar cheese

2 tablespoons butter

1 teaspoon hot sauce

3 bacon slices

1 pound medium shrimp, peeled and deveine

Kosher salt, to taste

Freshly ground black pepper, to taste

¼ cup all-purpose flour

2 garlic cloves, minced

Fresh lemon wedges, for garnish (optional)

In a medium saucepan, combine the water, 1¾ cups of the stock, and the cream; bring to a boil over medium-high heat. Gradually and slowly whisk in the grits. Reduce the heat to low, stirring, until only an occasional bubble breaks the surface. Simmer for 30 to 40 minutes, until grits are fully cooked. Add the cheese, butter, and ½ teaspoon hot sauce to the grits, stirring to combine. Reduce the heat to the lowest setting and keep the grits warm.

In a large skillet over medium-high heat, cook the bacon until crisp. Remove the bacon and drain on paper towels. Reserve about 1 tablespoon of drippings in the skillet. Crumble the bacon and set aside. Sprinkle the shrimp all over with salt and pepper; dredge in the flour. Add the shrimp and garlic to the bacon grease in the skillet and sauté 2 minutes, or until shrimp are light brown. Stir in the remaining chicken stock and hot sauce and cook 2 more minutes, gently scraping the bottom of the skillet with a spatula to loosen any particles that stick to the bottom of the skillet. Serve shrimp mixture over the warm cheese grits. Top with the crumbled bacon; serve immediately with lemon wedges on the side.

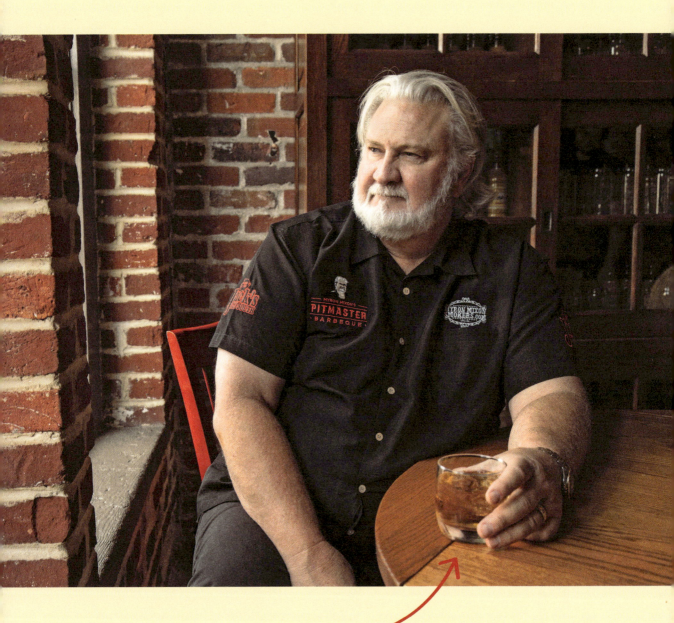

Only drink recipe I need: On the rocks.
Easy as a Sunday morning. Like me.

CHAPTER NINE

WHAT ELSE?

SIDES, DESSERTS, DRINKS

Championship
St. Louis Ribs
page 189

Skillet Cornbread
page 306

Pickles you get at my restaurant in Old Town Alexandria, Virginia. Damn good with your barbecue.

Myron's Mac 'n' Cheese page 308

What do you like to eat when you aren't eating barbecue?

That seems to be the million-dollar question. I mean, everyone asks me that. I'm not sure why. I'm the winningest man in barbecue. What difference does it make what I eat when I'm not standing at my pits? But I tell you what, since people seem to want to know: I happen to be a very good cook in the kitchen and not just at the smoker. On the opposite page is a personal recipe of mine that has nothing to do with barbecue and yet is a Myron Mixon original.

The follow-up to this question that a lot of folks ask me when I'm at contests and cooking demos: Where do I like to go out to eat? Answer: I happen to like Italian food. We don't have much of it in South Georgia, so when I get the chance I go for it. Earth-shattering, I know.

LOW-COUNTRY SHRIMP BOIL

SERVES 8 TO 10

As many of my fans already know, I offer barbecue cooking classes at my compound in South Georgia. The events last all weekend and we prep and smoke all the major competition categories during that time. On Friday nights I have a casual meet-and-greet party so the students can mingle with one another and with me. This is almost always what I like to serve—it's casual, it's distinctly Southern (it's a specialty of the Southeastern coast of the US, where it's sometimes also called Frogmore Stew), and it's damn tasty. I serve this with plenty of beer, coleslaw (page 297), tartar sauce, and cocktail sauce. This recipe is easily adjusted to feed either more or fewer people.

ingredients

2 pounds kielbasa or other smoked sausage

3 gallons water

1 cup Old Bay Seasoning

½ cup fresh lemon juice

2 teaspoons cayenne pepper

2 tablespoons kosher salt

4 heads garlic, peeled

16 to 20 small red new potatoes

4 large ears corn, husked and cut into thirds

5 pounds fresh shrimp in the shell (36- to 40-count), heads removed (about 8 to 9 ounces per person)

1 cup tartar sauce (optional)

1 cup cocktail sauce (optional)

3 lemons, quartered (optional)

Heat a large skillet over medium heat. Slice the sausage into 2-inch cubes and add to the skillet. Cook until well browned and cooked through, about 10 minutes. Set aside.

Place the water, Old Bay, lemon juice, cayenne, and salt in a very large pot and bring to a boil over high heat. Add the garlic and potatoes, return to a boil, reduce the heat, and simmer until the potatoes are tender, 10 to 15 minutes.

Toss in the corn. Bring the liquid back to a boil, lower the heat, and simmer for 10 minutes. Toss in the shrimp and boil for 2½ additional minutes, or until the shrimp are uniformly pink and cooked through. Turn off the heat and stir in the sausage. Drain immediately. To serve, cover a table with newspapers and dump the mixture out onto it or pile it in a large bowl and let guests help themselves. Serve with plenty of tartar sauce, cocktail sauce, and quartered fresh lemons, if you like.

What are the best Southern deviled eggs?

Deviled eggs are at the top of the list whenever anyone, I don't care who they are, decides to rank ultimate Southern foods. If you have a barbecue at your house and you want to give it that true Southern flavor, you ought to serve some deviled eggs. My version incorporates barbecue flavors, down to the leftover meat I stuff them with. If I don't have any leftover 'cue hanging around, I use a just a little of the meat that I'm going to be serving during the barbecue—all you need is 1 cup of smoked meat and you can make deviled eggs that'll blow away your friends.

PITMASTER-STYLE DEVILED EGGS

MAKES 1 DOZEN DEVILED EGGS

Every party I go to, there never seem to be enough deviled eggs. You might want to double up on this one.

ingredients

6 large eggs

1 teaspoon Dijon mustard

1 to 2 dashes hot sauce

1 tablespoon Jack's Old South Original Rub or make your own (see page 72), plus more for dusting

Kosher salt, to taste

Freshly ground black pepper, to taste

½ cup finely chopped smoked pork (page 162), smoked brisket (page 223), or smoked chicken (page 33)

¼ cup mayonnaise

1 tablespoon pickle relish (optional)

Rinse the eggs with warm water and place in a small saucepan. Cover with cold water, place the pan over medium-high heat, and bring to a boil. Turn off the heat, cover, and let sit for 10 to 12 minutes. Drain, rinse under cold water, and peel. Cool in the refrigerator, loosely covered, for 15 minutes.

Halve the eggs lengthwise, and carefully scoop out the yolks. Place the yolks in a bowl and mash with a fork. Add the mustard, hot sauce, rub, salt, and pepper, and barbecue meat. Stir to combine. Finally, stir in the mayonnaise.

Fill each egg white with about 1½ teaspoons of the egg yolk mixture and dust the top with a little more rub. Arrange in a spoke design on a platter or in a deviled egg plate. Garnish with a dab of pickle relish, if you like.

Do you make Brunswick Stew out of squirrel?

Brunswick Stew is one of those extremely old-fashioned Southern foods, like grits or collards or fried green tomatoes. The only difference is that it's got a lower profile. And there's a reason for that: Brunswick Stew was traditionally made with whatever wild game a Southerner had on hand (it could've been a squirrel in some cases, I'm sure) and was designed to use broth and vegetables (and we're not talking kale or butternut squash; we're talking potatoes and corn and lima beans) to stretch the meat to feed as many people as possible. There's a battle in the South about who invented Brunswick Stew—it's either from Brunswick, Georgia, or from Brunswick County, Virginia, and both areas lay heavy claim to it. The origins don't matter as much as what's in the bowl because either way, this humble classic will warm you up. I know that rabbit or chicken and sometimes even squirrel are the traditional meats used in Brunswick Stew. But oftentimes I've been known to make it richer and more interesting by substituting brisket. That's right: You can substitute 3 cups of finely shredded smoked brisket (page 235) in place of the whole chicken. Just add it to your pot when you pour in the broth, and you'll have my BBQ-style Brunswick Stew, meatier than the original but still made in the spirit of the South. The only difficult part is that it will require considerable restraint to save 3 cups of shredded brisket. Then again, you could always smoke a small brisket just for this purpose if you felt like it.

BRUNSWICK STEW

SERVES 6 TO 8 (MAIN-COURSE SERVINGS)

Roy Blount, Jr. got it right when he said, "Brunswick Stew is what happens when small mammals carrying ears of corn fall into barbecue pits."

ingredients

1 (3-pound) whole chicken, cut into 8 or 10 pieces

Kosher salt, to taste

Freshly ground black pepper, to taste

1 cup all-purpose flour

1 teaspoon cayenne pepper

4 tablespoons vegetable oil

1 medium yellow onion, chopped

1 bay leaf

2 cups chicken broth

1 28-ounce can chopped tomatoes

1 10-ounce package frozen corn

1 10-ounce package frozen lima beans

Use paper towels or a clean kitchen towel to pat the chicken dry all over. Sprinkle the chicken pieces evenly with salt and pepper.

Whisk together the flour and cayenne in a shallow bowl, then dredge the chicken pieces through the seasoned flour, shaking off any excess.

Heat 2 tablespoons oil in a wide 6- to 7-quart heavy pot over medium heat until it shimmers. Brown half of the chicken pieces, turning once, about 10 minutes total. Transfer to a plate. Add 1 tablespoon oil to the pot and brown the remaining chicken pieces; transfer to a plate.

Add remaining tablespoon oil to the pot along with the onion; season to taste with salt and pepper and cook, stirring and scraping up brown bits, until the onion is softened, about 8 minutes.

Add the bay leaf, broth, tomatoes, and the chicken pieces with any meat juices from the plate and bring to a simmer. Simmer, covered, 50 minutes.

Stir in the corn and lima beans, then simmer, uncovered, until the stew is slightly thickened and the vegetables are tender, 15 to 20 minutes. Season with salt and pepper. Discard the bay leaf.

Serve warm in bowls with cornbread (page 306) on the side if you like.

Q:

What's the secret to
your coleslaw?

A:

I love it when people ask me advice about coleslaw. Have you ever stopped to think about why coleslaw exists? Lucky for you, I have. Coleslaw exists to complement barbecue. It exists to add a bite of fresh, tart flavor and crisp texture to smoky meat. That sounds like a simple job, but it's far from it. Even though coleslaw has one purpose, I happen to believe that there is not a one-size-fits-all coleslaw recipe that will work with every Southern dish or every type of barbecue. That's why I'm giving you two foolproof coleslaw recipes here. One creamy version to go with your fried foods and soul food dishes, and one specifically to serve with your smoked barbecued meats.

CLASSIC CREAMY COLESLAW

MAKES 10 TO 12 SIDE-DISH SERVINGS

This is the slaw my mama made and is probably still my favorite. Creamy slaws like this are excellent with fried chicken or fried fish. This should be well chilled and served cold.

ingredients

1 large head green cabbage, or 2 small heads, coarsely chopped

2 medium sweet onions, such as Vidalia, diced

2 ripe tomatoes, diced

3 cups mayonnaise

2 teaspoons apple cider vinegar

Kosher salt, to taste

Freshly ground black pepper, to taste

In a large bowl, combine all of the ingredients. Toss thoroughly. You should prepare this the day before or at least 6 hours before you plan to serve it. Store it covered in the refrigerator. When you're ready to serve it, drain the slaw in a large colander. Toss it again thoroughly and add more salt and pepper to taste.

RED CABBAGE SLAW

MAKES 10 SERVINGS

Prepare this slaw one day in advance of serving, then drain it and season with more salt and pepper before bringing it to the table. Its sweet-and-savory bite pairs great with smoky meats.

ingredients

½ cup peanut oil

⅔ cup red wine vinegar

1 teaspoon teriyaki sauce

2 tablespoons sugar

1 teaspoon kosher salt

¼ teaspoon onion powder

¼ teaspoon garlic powder

½ tablespoon ground black pepper

1 large head red cabbage, shredded

In a bowl, whisk together all the ingredients except the cabbage. When everything is well blended, add the cabbage and toss. Cover the slaw and refrigerate overnight. Drain before serving.

Q:

How do you make good potato salad?

A:

I reckon people ask me about how to make good potato salad a lot because on one of the seasons of *BBQ Pitmasters*, we had a potato salad challenge. And I guess I had a lot to say about potato salad and how to make a good one. The judging panel consisted of NFL football superstar Warren Sapp, celebrity chef Art Smith, and yours truly. So on this particular episode when we held a competition for the best homemade potato salad, I said to the contestants: "You've got to have mayonnaise to have a good potato salad." I pride myself on my potato salad, and that's what I believe: I don't care what else you put in it—to be good, it's got to be a little bit creamy.

CLASSIC SOUTHERN POTATO SALAD

2 pounds red-skin new potatoes

1 cup sour cream

1 teaspoon dried dill

½ teaspoon garlic powder

½ teaspoon onion powder

⅓ cup chopped fresh chives

1 cup mayonnaise

1 tablespoon kosher salt

1 tablespoon freshly ground black pepper

6 hard-boiled eggs, coarsely chopped

¼ cup Jack's Old South Original Rub or make your own (see page 72), for garnish (optional)

Wash the potatoes well. In a large heavy pot, add enough water to cover the potatoes. Bring water to a boil. Add the potatoes and boil for 15 to 20 minutes, or until they are tender, being careful not to overcook them, as you don't want them mushy.

Drain the potatoes in a colander and run cold water over them to stop them from continuing to cook. Let them cool in the colander.

Slice the potatoes into thin rounds, leaving the skin on. Set aside.

In a medium bowl, combine the sour cream, dill, garlic powder, onion powder, chives, mayonnaise, salt, and pepper. Stir well.

In a large bowl, toss the potatoes with the eggs and the sour cream dressing. Cover the bowl and chill in the refrigerator for 2 hours before serving. Sprinkle the barbecue rub all over the top of the potato salad before serving, if you like.

Q:

What's the secret to your baked beans?

A:

I'm not sure why baked beans are so often referred to as "Boston baked beans," but I'd guess that it has to do with the Pilgrims and the fact that the beans usually have molasses in them, and also salt pork. They may have come up with the recipe for baked beans in colonial New England, but to me they're permanently associated with the South—where we eat them all the time with our barbecue. As for me, I like sweetening my baked beans with peaches—and I'm not ashamed to admit that I'm talking about canned peaches, because their juices go well with the beans and with the barbecue I serve right next to them on the plate.

PEACH BAKED BEANS

MAKES 8 SIDE-DISH SERVINGS

You can make these beans in the oven or in the smoker. They're unique, and I mean that in a good way.

ingredients

½ cup ketchup

½ cup pure maple syrup

¼ cup Dijon mustard

3 cups canned peach pie filling

1 teaspoon apple cider vinegar

1 (7-ounce) jar diced pimiento peppers, drained

¼ cup light brown sugar, packed

Kosher salt, to taste

Freshly ground black pepper, to taste

Four (16-ounce) cans Bush's baked beans, rinsed and drained

In a saucepan, combine all the ingredients except the salt, pepper, and beans. Bring the sauce to a boil, whisking to dissolve the sugar. Reduce the heat to moderately low and simmer until reduced by one-third, about 20 minutes. Season with salt and pepper.

To make it in the oven: Preheat the oven to 325°F. Pour the sauce and the beans into a large enameled cast-iron casserole dish and stir to combine. Cover partially and bake for 1 hour, until the beans are glazed. Taste the beans and season with salt and pepper, then serve.

To make it in a smoker: Heat the smoker to 325°F. Pour the sauce and beans into a large deep aluminum baking pan. Cover the pan with foil. Cook in the smoker until the beans are tender, checking to make sure they're not drying out, about 1 hour. The beans are done when the top is dark brown and the sauce is bubbling. Let the beans stand in their pan, covered, for about 15 minutes to rest before serving.

What's your secret for making good collards?

I've been making and eating collard greens for what seems like my whole life. Southern gardeners have been growing collard greens for generations, as this leafy and hardy vegetable grows all over the place down here and thrives in the cool weather of our autumns and early springs. We cook them with pork to lend them some good flavor and fat, and also some sheen: We like our collards shiny and bright.

SMOKY COLLARD GREENS

You need to wash collard greens thoroughly before you cook them. Serve them with hot sauce, if you like. And if you have leftover collards, reheat a portion and then slide a poached or fried egg on top for a mighty fine breakfast.

ingredients

1 (½-pound) piece salt pork or meaty slab bacon, or jowl meat if you have it

1 gallon water

1 teaspoon garlic powder

1 tablespoon kosher salt

1 teaspoon freshly ground black pepper

4 tablespoons (½ stick) unsalted butter

1 tablespoon Accent Flavor Enhancer or, if you're uncomfortable cooking with MSG, substitute seasoned salt or Bragg's Liquid Amino Acids

1 teaspoon smoked paprika

3½ to 4 pounds collard greens, stems discarded, leaves cut into 1-inch-long strips

In a large pot, cook the bacon over moderately high heat, turning, until it is golden all over, about 4 minutes. Add the water and bring to a boil. Add garlic powder, salt, and pepper and simmer over low heat until the bacon is fork-tender, about 45 minutes.

Bring the liquid to a vigorous boil. Stir in the butter, Accent, and paprika. Add large handfuls of the collards at a time, allowing each batch to wilt slightly before adding more. Return the liquid to a boil. Reduce the heat and simmer the collards over moderate heat, stirring occasionally, until they are tender, about 30 minutes.

Transfer the bacon to a plate, then cut off and discard the skin and fat. Using two forks, shred the meat and return it to the pot. Using tongs, transfer the collards and bacon to bowls, dividing both evenly. Spoon some of the liquid over the greens and serve.

Q:

*what kind of cornbread
do you like?*

A:

This is a question I appreciate, because there are a lot of kinds of cornbread out there, and some of them are just not worthy of the name "cornbread." Cornbread is not something that has flavors, folks: It's not jalapeño-cheddar or mozzarella–sundried tomato, or blueberry-sage. Cornbread is supposed to taste like corn, which is to say a little sweet, a little salty—it has its own mild flavor, and that's why we love it. Southern cooks have been making cornbread probably since the beginning of time—or at least our time here. Corn is cheap, plentiful, and easy to grind, and that's why we all had plenty of grits and cornbread. I like to make my cornbread in a cast-iron skillet because that's how my grandmothers did it. It ensures the cornbread will have a nice crisp crunch on the outside while it stays moist and soft inside.

SKILLET CORNBREAD

MAKES 16 WEDGES OF CORNBREAD

ingredients

1¼ cup yellow cornmeal

1¼ cup all-purpose flour

1 tablespoon sugar

1½ teaspoons baking powder

½ teaspoon baking soda

1 tablespoon kosher salt

1 large egg, lightly beaten

1¾ cup buttermilk

4 tablespoons unsalted butter

Preheat the oven to 425°F.

In a large mixing bowl, whisk together the cornmeal, flour, sugar, baking powder, baking soda, and salt; set aside. In a small bowl, whisk together the egg and buttermilk; stir into the flour mixture.

Over medium heat, melt the butter in a 10-inch cast-iron skillet (or substitute a 2-quart baking dish, heavily greased). Remove skillet from the heat, swirling the melted butter to coat the bottom of the skillet. Pour in the batter. Bake until a cake tester comes out clean, 20 to 25 minutes. Remove the cornbread from the oven and let it cool slightly, about 10 minutes.

Cut into wedges and serve warm, or cool completely and serve at room temperature, with more cold butter and honey on the side, if you like.

Q:

what's your best
mac 'n' cheese tip?

A:

The first thing you need to know about this recipe is that Southern-style macaroni and cheese is about one thing. It ain't the cheese you use, which does not need to be fancy. And it sure isn't about adding anything like truffle oil or basil oil. It's about butter. That's right; it's about buttery noodles and making them as delicious as possible with a little cheese sauce. To me, mac 'n' cheese is not something that comes in some pretty little Le Creuset ramekin with a side of grated Parmesan. It's served in a gigantic aluminum baking pan right between the baked beans and the potato salad. It should be hearty and comforting, rich and simple. Here's the way I like to do it:

MYRON'S MAC 'N' CHEESE

MAKES 6 SIDE-DISH SERVINGS

ingredients

4 tablespoons (½ stick) unsalted butter, softened

Kosher salt, to taste

1 pound elbow macaroni

2 tablespoons all-purpose flour

3 cups milk

2½ cups grated sharp cheddar cheese

Freshly ground black pepper, to taste

Use 2 tablespoons of the butter to generously grease a 13 by 9-inch baking pan all over the bottom and sides.

Over medium-high heat, bring a large heavy pot of well-salted water—you want the water to be salty like the sea—to a boil. Add the macaroni, lower the heat to a simmer, and cook according to the package directions for al dente. When the pasta is finished cooking, drain it in a colander, run it under cold water to stop it from cooking any further, and set it aside.

In a large saucepan over medium heat, melt the remaining 2 tablespoons of butter. When the butter is just melted, sprinkle the flour into the pan and cook, whisking the flour into the butter, for about 1 minute, or until the butter and flour form a blond paste. Slowly and little by little, whisk in the milk, taking plenty of time to whisk between additions of milk, until all the milk is whisked into the paste and a smooth sauce remains. While whisking, bring the mixture up to a simmer so that it's just beginning to bubble, then remove the saucepan from the heat and whisk in 2 cups of the shredded cheese. When all the cheese has melted into the sauce, season with salt and pepper to taste.

Preheat the broiler.

Add the drained macaroni into the sauce and stir to combine. Transfer the macaroni and cheese into the prepared pan. Scatter the remaining shredded cheese over the top of the mac 'n' cheese. Put the pan in the broiler and cook until the cheese is golden brown on top, checking frequently, 3 to 5 minutes. Remove the pan from the broiler and let stand for 10 minutes before serving.

Q:

Do you drink when you're cooking?

A:

I make no secret of the fact that I like to drink Crown Royal Canadian Whisky.[*] **I have loved Crown for as long as I can remember, but let's just say for as long as I've been able to afford to drink it.** I love the soft purple bag it comes in. I love the fact that the top of the bottle is a little gold crown. I love the smoothness of it. I love it when I meet barbecue lovers who know enough about me to bring me bottles of the stuff. But you know what I don't love? Anyone who comes to work wasted. Winning competitions by cooking the world's best barbecue is my job, and just like you don't drink on your job—I hope you don't, anyway—I don't drink on mine. So please forgive me if I don't take a shot with you or have a beer in my hand when you see me at Memphis in May or the Giant BBQ Battle or the American Royal. I'm there to win, and one thing that has always separated me from many of my competitors is that I'm not at a barbecue contest to party. I'm there to smoke some meat, win some money, and get the hell on the road to the next one. I'll have a drink when the judging's done.

---

[*] If you're curious about what I drink when I'm not drinking Crown, I happen to like Stella Artois. Damn good beer. And I've been working with the good people who make Cabo Wabo Tequila for a few years now, and they make a mighty fine product as well.

Q:

Can I smoke dessert?

A:

One thing people might not realize about pitmasters is that we're chefs. We don't just function to cook outside over fires. In fact, to do what we do well, we have to study and practice, just like all professional cooks. I love experimenting with recipes in the kitchen—indoors and outdoors—and I do it as much as I can. One thing I've experimented with over the years is cooking dessert outside. I asked myself which desserts might benefit from a slight enhancement of smoky flavor. I came up with just two. But the good news is that they're both excellent. And if you've already got your smoker all fired up (or your gas grill or charcoal grill), then you won't have to turn on your oven at all that day.

CHOCOLATE CAKE ON THE GRILL

SERVES 8 TO 10

ingredients

FOR THE CAKE:

2 cups all-purpose flour

½ cup unsweetened cocoa powder

½ tablespoon baking powder

½ teaspoon baking soda

½ teaspoon kosher salt

¾ cup (1½ sticks) unsalted butter, softened

2 cups sugar

3 large eggs

3 ounces semisweet chocolate, melted and cooled

2 teaspoons pure vanilla extract

¾ cup sour cream

FOR THE CHOCOLATE GLAZE:

½ cup sugar

¼ cup water

1 tablespoon unsweetened cocoa powder

1 teaspoon vanilla extract

OPTIONAL GARNISHES:

Whipped cream

Fruit

3 slices crumbled bacon

If it ain't hot already, heat your smoker (or charcoal grill or gas grill) to medium heat.

Generously grease a 10-cup Bundt pan.

In a medium bowl, sift the flour with the cocoa, baking powder, baking soda, and salt. In a large bowl using an electric mixer, beat the butter with the sugar until pale and fluffy 3 to 5 minutes. Add the eggs, one at a time, beating well after each addition. Add the melted chocolate and vanilla and beat until the batter is smooth. Beat in the dry ingredients in 3 batches, alternating with the sour cream and beginning and ending with the flour; beat until just combined.

Scrape the batter into the prepared pan and use a rubber spatula to smooth the surface.

Place the cake pan on the grill and cover. Let it cook for 45 minutes to 1 hour, until a tester inserted in the center comes out with moist crumbs attached. Remove from the grill or oven and let the cake rest in the pan to cool completely, about 1 hour.

While the cake is cooking, make the glaze: In a medium saucepan, combine the sugar and water and bring to a boil; stir to dissolve the sugar. Whisk in the cocoa and vanilla and let cool.

Invert the cake onto a serving platter. Brush a thin layer of the glaze over the cake and let dry slightly, about 2 minutes. Repeat 3 more times, letting the glaze dry slightly for 2 minutes before brushing a new layer on. Cut into wedges and serve with whipped cream and fruit, or if you're like me and you love bacon, add a little crumbled bacon on top, too.

Note: You can make this cake in the oven. Preheat it to 350°F, and bake it for 45 minutes to an hour, following the instructions as given.

SMOKED BLACKBERRY COBBLER

This is a great thing to throw into your smoker after you're finished barbecuing your meats. Just stoke your heat a little longer and you'll have one of my all-time favorite desserts. I have blackberry bushes in my front yard; I love them so much.

ingredients

FOR THE CAKE:

5 cups fresh blackberries

½ cup sugar

1 tablespoon quick-cooking tapioca

¼ teaspoon salt

2 teaspoons grated fresh ginger, or 1 teaspoon ground ginger

FOR THE TOPPING:

¾ cup crushed shortbread cookies (about 12 cookies)

⅓ cup all-purpose flour

3 tablespoons light brown sugar

2 tablespoons unsalted butter, cut into small cubes

OPTIONAL GARNISHES:

Whipped cream

Ice cream

Make the filling: In a large nonreactive bowl, combine the blackberries, sugar, tapioca, salt, and ginger. Pour the mixture into a 2-quart disposable foil pan. Cover the pan tightly with aluminum foil.

Make the topping: In the bowl of a food processor, combine the cookies, flour, and brown sugar. Pulse to combine. Add the cubes of butter and pulse until the butter is in small pea-size bits and the topping has the consistency of coarsely ground meal; set aside.

Heat your smoker to 275°F.

Place the foil pan on a rack in the center of the smoker and smoke for 30 minutes. After 30 minutes of steady smoking your cobbler at 275°F, remove it from the smoker, uncover it, and sprinkle the topping evenly over the top of the cobbler. Cover the cobbler again with the foil, loosely this time. Smoke the cobbler for 10 to 15 minutes, or until the mixture is bubbly and the fruit has thickened. Remove the cobbler from the smoker and let it cool, loosely covered, on a wire rack for 20 minutes. Serve warm, topped with whipped cream or ice cream, if you like.

BANANA PUDDING

MAKES 6 SERVINGS

For the record, in case you were wondering, my favorite dessert that does not need to be smoked or grilled, ever, happens to be banana pudding. Here's the simplest and tastiest way to make it, classic Southern-style. And yes, I call for Nilla wafers, and no, no other brand will do.

ingredients

5 large egg yolks

¼ cup cornstarch

⅓ cup sugar

Dash of kosher salt

2 cups whole milk (do not use skim)

2 tablespoons unsalted cold butter

2 teaspoons vanilla extract

18 Nilla wafer cookies, coarsely crushed

3 ripe bananas, thinly sliced

In a medium bowl, whisk the egg yolks with the cornstarch, the sugar, and salt. In a medium saucepan over medium heat, gradually bring the milk to a boil. Gradually whisk the milk into the egg yolks until smooth. Transfer the pudding mixture to the saucepan. Cook over moderate heat, whisking, until the pudding is thick, about 3 minutes. Scrape the pudding into a bowl and whisk in the cold butter and vanilla. Cover with plastic wrap and refrigerate until chilled, at least 4 hours, or overnight.

When you're ready to serve the pudding: Spoon the pudding into six bowls. Garnish with the thinly sliced bananas and sprinkle all over with the crushed Nilla wafers. Serve cold, right away.

Note: You can serve the cookies without crushing them—just allow three per bowl. You can also add a couple tablespoons of banana or almond liqueur (or a combination of a both) into the pudding mixture right after you transfer it to the saucepan.

LEMON CHESS PIE

All right I'll give you one more dessert, because y'all know I love dessert, and I know you all love it, too. This one also does not get cooked in the smoker or grill. Instead, this pie is extremely popular at my restaurant Myron Mixon's Pitmaster Barbecue in the historic Old Town area of Alexandria, Virginia. It's another classic Southern dessert, a custard-based pie flavored with fresh lemon, and it'll be right at home in your backyard.

ingredients

FOR THE CRUST:

1½ cups all-purpose flour

¼ teaspoon salt

¼ teaspoon baking powder

¼ cup vegetable shortening

¼ cup cold butter, cut into very small dice

1 teaspoon apple cider vinegar

4 tablespoons ice water

FOR THE FILLING:

6 tablespoons butter, melted

1⅔ cups sugar

¾ cup fresh lemon juice (juice from about 3 large lemons)

½ teaspoon salt

1 tablespoon cornmeal

1 tablespoon plus 1 teaspoon cornstarch

5 large eggs, beaten to combine

Make the crust: Whisk together all of the dry ingredients. Using two knives or a pastry dough cutter, work in the shortening until it's well combined. Mix the small butter pieces into the dough to evenly distribute them. Sprinkle the vinegar and the water over the dough while tossing it together with a fork. As soon as the dough becomes cohesive and you can squeeze it into a ball easily, stop mixing; there should still be visible pieces of butter in the dough. Add up to 2 additional tablespoons water, if necessary, to make the dough come together. Flatten the dough into a disk and wrap it in plastic wrap. Refrigerate for at least 1 hour. When you're ready to make the crust, let it rest for about 5 minutes at room temperature before rolling. Roll the dough to a 12 to 13-inch circle, and settle it gently into a 9-inch pie pan; the pan shouldn't be more than 1½ inches deep. Flute or crimp the edge of the crust as desired. Place the crust in the refrigerator (no need to cover it) while you make the filling.

Preheat the oven to 375°F.

Make the filling: Stir together the melted butter and sugar, then mix in the remaining filling ingredients. Whisk until well combined. Pour the filling into the chilled pie shell. Bake the pie on the bottom shelf of the preheated oven for 45 to 50 minutes, or until the center is set. The top should be golden brown. Remove the pie from the oven and allow it to cool before cutting and serving.

INDEX

Index

317

Library of Congress Control Number: 2018936225

ISBN: 978-1-4197-2702-3
eISBN: 978-1-68335-503-8

Printed and bound in the United States
10 9 8 7 6 5 4 3 2 1

Abrams books are available at special discounts when purchased in quantity
for premiums and promotions as well as fundraising or educational use.
Special editions can also be created to specification. For details, contact
specialsales@abramsbooks.com or the address below.

Abrams® is a registered trademark of Harry N. Abrams, Inc.

ABRAMS The Art of Books
195 Broadway, New York, NY 10007
abramsbooks.com